My Kind of Town

Issue One

Haymarket and Fitzalan Square in 1966. Did you ever visit Davy's Mikado Cafe shown in the foreground?

Mike Firth & John Firminger have asserted their right under the Copyright, Designs and Patents Act 1988 to be identified as the authors of this work.

With grateful thanks to all contributors including Bobby Knutt, Dave Berry, Neil Anderson, Margaret Shaw, Michael Liversidge, Arthur Firth, Sybil O'Brien and Dafydd Manton.

Published by Heron Publications Ltd, 2011.   ISBN 978-0-9564825-2-5
Typeset and Designed by Heron Publications Ltd, 24 Hutcliffe Wood Road, Beauchief, Sheffield, S8 0EX.

Cover design: Helen Firth.   Proof reading: Kat Withers.

The authors and publishers have made all reasonable attempts to contact copyright holders for permission to use images.

DO YOU REMEMBER?

SEE HOW MANY OF THESE YOU CAN RECALL

THE 'RAG & TAG'
S.U.T.
MARY GENTLE'S, HOWARD ST.
'BIG ADA'
AQUARIUS NIGHT CLUB
CO-OP HALL, FRECHEVILLE
HOT PIE SHOP, DUKE STREET
OGLEY'S PET SHOP
EL MAMBO
VIOLET MAY'S
HIGHCLIFFE HOTEL FOLK CLUB
ROYAL HOSPITAL
STANLEY ST. CLUB AUDITIONS
MYER'S TRIPE STALL
B.R.S. DEPOT, STANIFORTH ROAD
CRANE'S, LADY'S BRIDGE
THE BARLEYCORN, CAMBRIDGE ST.
CORPORATION ST. BATHS
FARM GROUND'S FAIR
TAGGY'S ICE CREAM
NORTON AIR-SHOW
WILKES HARDWARE SHOP, NORFOLK ST.
RED CIRCLE LIBRARY
THE BLACKSMITH, SYCAMORE ST.
RICKSAW CHINESE RESTAURANT
SHADES NIGHT CLUB
HARRY BENDON
WALSH'S DEPARTMENT STORE
LIGHT FANTASTIC (Band)
CARLTON CINEMA, ARBOURTHORNE
THE PINK UN'
DOWN BROADWAY
BROCKLEHURST MOTORS
HYDE PARK DOG-TRACK
SHEAF VALLEY BATHS
'POND ST. NORA'
VICTORIA STATION
TEENAGE TAVERN
TURNER'S NEWS

SWOP SHOPS
SIDEWALK COFFEE BAR
SATURDAY MORNING MATINEES
CAVENDISH/BAILEY'S/ROMEO & JULIET'S
NIGHT CLUBS
THREE CRANE'S FOLK CLUB
DAVY'S SHOPS
OLD SWEET FACTORY, SHREWSBURY RD.
THE STONE HOUSE, CHURCH ST.
BSM DRIVING SCHOOL, QUEEN'S RD.
UNIVERSITY RAG PARADE
CHANGE ALLEY
RON DELTA
DAINTY'S SWEET SHOPS
SNOW WHITE LAUNDRY
ATTERCLIFFE ROLLER RINK
'RECORD YOUR OWN VOICE' BOOTH, (POND
ST. BUS STATION)
TERRY STEEPLES
WOODEN STILTS
BARNEY GOODMAN'S
THE SUN SOUND CLUB
OFF-LICENSES
WINTER WARMERS
ISLAMABAD RESTAURANT
BROOK SHAWS
TOUCH BURNERS
WHITSUNTIDE CLOTHES
BENDI-BUS
WILSON GUMPERT'S TOY SHOP
AZENA BALLROOM, GLEADLESS
REDGATES
HEINZ FOODS, SHALESMOOR
ARMY RECRUITMENT CENTRE, HAYMARKET
GLEN DALE & THE CANDIES
NETHER EDGE JAZZ
SHEFFIELD ABBATOIR
WIGFALLS
UNIT 19 RECORDING STUDIOS

Read all about it

WELCOME to the new publication looking at old Sheffield.

The dictionary tells us that 'nostalgia' is a sentimental yearning for the past - and that is really what 'My Kind of Town' is all about.

If you've already had a flick through the pages of this first issue, you will hopefully have spotted a thing or two to give you warm memories of days gone by. Now make a cuppa, put your feet up and really wallow in our reflections of bygone Sheffield.

Something the dictionary doesn't mention is that one of the best things about nostalgia is being able to share it with others. We all have memories of bygone days, people, events and buildings and this magazine positively encourages you to share your recollections with other readers.

Whether you can recall growing up in Sheffield during the war, you have fond memories of meeting someone special at Cole's Corner, you remember travelling on a 'bendy bus' or you once ran a business down the Hole in the Road, we want to hear from you.

Memories are best served up with illustrations too, so raid your loft and cupboard drawers to share some of your special photographs with other readers.

We want to hear about your school days, your first job, your favourite shop, your first car, a band you once played in... anything at all really! If you feel the urge to go on a personal nostalgia trip, 'My Kind of Town' should be your destination.

Are you planning a school reunion? Is there someone from years ago who you would dearly like to trace? Contact us and we will do our best to help.

Mike Firth and John Firminger are joint editors of this magazine and although they love turning back the clock, sometimes their memories aren't what they once were and they may get a little carried away with their recollections. If, after reading an article, you think you know better than our two - or you may simply have something to add - please get in touch.

The really good news is that by the time you have read all the way to the end of this first edition of our new publication, issue two will be just around the corner. 'My Kind of Town' is to be published four times a year and we look forward to having you on board from now onwards.

My Kind of Town is produced by Heron Publications Ltd, 24 Hutcliffe Wood Road, Beauchief, Sheffield, S8 OEX, and is printed by Buxton Press. Editors: Mike Firth & John Firminger. Design: Helen Firth. Telephone 0114 2357777. Email: mike@heronpublications.co.uk Material is copyright and should not be reproduced without permission. Views expressed by individual contributors and advertisers are not necessarily those of the publishers.

The city with a hole in the middle

Long before Sheffield city centre welcomed its 'Sugar Cube', it used to have a 'Wedding Cake' and an 'Egg Box' too. For a couple of decades, however, arguably the city's most famous landmark was the 'Hole in the Road'. In its heyday this spectacular subway was a place to meet and greet and even eat. There were shops down there, floral displays and the biggest, meanest tropical fish you could wish to see. You could disappear from sight down an escalator on High Street and moments later pop up on Arundel Gate or Angel Street or outside C&A. But it wasn't always that way. Often the escalator you required was broken and as the years went by the bright flowers gave way to drab graffiti.

NOW part of Sheffield folklore, this unique piece of construction will always be affectionately known as the 'Hole in the Road'.

Officially named 'Castle Square' it was built in the area which was originally known as the Market Place or The Shambles. Many buildings in this area were damaged or destroyed on the night of 12th December, 1940, when German aircraft bombed Sheffield. The bomb sites were cleared but most remained empty for many years.

In 1968 many old streets were cleared to make way for the new Arundel Gate, a swish dual carriageway road that terminated at a large roundabout built on the former market place. Underneath was a network of underpasses and shops with a central circular area open to the sky.

Someone who was at the official opening of the development was Keith Strong, then a young reporter for 'The Star'.

"What I do remember is thinking how surreal it was," he recalls. "Someone had created a giant pot-hole in the city centre. I never conveyed my thoughts into print, but I was amused to consider what the reaction would be if it was mysteriously filled in overnight... or traffic kept being swallowed up by it... or it turned into some subterranean fantasy land with strange creatures roaming about and picking off passers-by, winos, etc.

"My overall feeling was that undesirables would be at home there and it could be a dangerous place to negotiate after dark."

Jarvis Cocker recalls being taken to the Hole in the Road to look at the fishtank as a reward for not causing too much trouble during a shopping expedition.

He says: "The Hole in the Road was one of my favourite places in Sheffield and I would always show it to any out-of-town visitors. I was dismayed when it was knocked down and filled in, in the early '90s.

"When I go back to Sheffield and see the mini-roundabout that now occupies its space I always find myself thinking about the fish in the fish tank and what happened to them. Maybe they're still down there in the dark; wondering where all the people have gone.

"The Hole in the Road also had a reputation for late-night

All things bright and beautiful...
Sheffielders are thrilled with their new
Hole in the Road landmark, bedecked in
colourful blooms

What a Hole... A dull, dismal and
depressing scene below ground level
shortly before the city's landmark was
closed and filled in

violence which made it a scary place to walk home through in the early hours. This was not helped at all by the fact that the building's construction gave rise to an effect similar to that of the Whispering Gallery in St Paul's Cathedral - meaning that it was extremely difficult to work out where any menacing noises were coming from."

John Firminger recalls the scene just prior to the development opening: "Before, it was a fairly precarious walk in between all the road and construction works around a somewhat awkward junction as the top of where Angel Street joined High Street. With a constantly busy pedestrian crossing and heavy traffic, the policeman on traffic duty always seemed to have his work cut out and the subway certainly alleviated a lot of the problems that incurred."

John's first venture into the 'Hole in the Road' was the day after it was opened in 1967.

"I made my way down the slope to the subway at the side of The Marples Hotel and on entering the large circular area, I was amazed by its concept with all the subways with shops in them

and, of course, the large fishtank.

"Following my nose, up through the open-air area and then down along another subway, I wondered where in fact it would bring me out. I was pleasantly surprised when it brought me out half-way down Angel Street by the Co-op, which was exactly the direction I wanted to be.

"A few months later I was with some friends from London and taking them down into the subway, they were amazed and impressed by its concept as they'd never seen anything like it."

John also recalls some of Castle Square's subterranean shops: "There was Turner News where I'd usually call in every day on my way home. Some of the other shops I'd frequent were Blaskey's Decorators, Bunker & Pratley's basement and the YEB shop."

Although considered by many to be a major city landmark, like many constructions of its time, it did not age well and was very dilapidated by the early 1990s. It lasted from 1967 until 1994, allegedly being filled in with the rubble from the demolished Hyde Park Flats.

Hot chestnuts, dancing dogs and all that jazz

TODAY, Snig Hill remains a main gateway out of the city but the once busy thoroughfare is now a shadow of its former self. Up to the late 1960s it was a thriving area, sporting numerous shops, businesses and homes that lined each side of the road.

Its curious name derived from a block of wood or a 'snig' which would be pushed under a cart-wheel to stop it running away downhill when the road was of a much steeper gradient than it became over the years. This would, of course, apply in older times when horse-pulled carts and carriages would be the common mode of transport.

From those now far-off times, pictures of Snig Hill show some dilapidated old timber-framed buildings where a few shops operated and the Castle pub which stood on the corner of Snig Hill, Water Lane and Castle Street. Boots the Chemist also had premises at the bottom before all were demolished to make way for the Corporation Buildings in 1904.

For around a hundred years, or just over, the Snig Hill and West Bar area was a hive of activity and entertainment, possibly like the West Street area is today. It was infested with pubs and taverns plus theatres and music halls such as The Gaiety, The Blue Boar and the largest, The Grand.

The original building that housed the Don Cinema is still standing at West Bar (now storage facilities) and is a hark back to my boyhood days when I often went there with my Grandma. I recall once seeing a singing dog performing on stage!

At the top left of Snig Hill, two pubs originally stood with the first being The Black Lion and then next door, The Black Swan. Standing tall, The Black Lion was severely damaged in The Blitz with The Black Swan also losing some of its upper two floors. Down the side of it was a passage that ran from Snig Hill through to cobbled lane at the back. After some post-war alterations, The Black Lion continued to operate as a single-storey public house and was a very popular hostelry right up to the early 1960s when it was demolished for re-development.

Across the road, at the bottom, Wilson Gumpert's toy shop was originally located here before moving to Fitzalan Square, with a sweet shop next door.

During the night of The Blitz on 12th December, 1940, Snig Hill was close to much of the bombing but managed to escape a lot of it. However, the top section of Corporation buildings was badly damaged and for safety reasons had to be demolished.

The following morning Snig Hill was a scene of chaos, strewn with debris and property as one former resident Alan Doughty recalled: "I can remember us going in the house and there were no windows in at all. Everything was covered in soot; it was really shocking."

Outside, things were just as bad, although some of the items strewn across the street included things like cricket balls and toys which had been blown out of Wilson Gumpert's toy shop and Suggs' Sports Shop.

In the 1970s, half of the remaining flats in Corporation Buildings were also demolished to make way for the South Yorkshire Police HQ. Across the road, the Probation Service offices replaced old shops and businesses, thus an ideal theme song for this re-development would possibly be 'I Fought The Law (And The Law Won)'!

Various traffic systems have left Snig Hill a quieter location and mainly a route for buses today.

Also contributing towards its past hustle and bustle was the small triangular-shaped bus station located at the bottom of Snig Hill, in Bridge Street, which provided transport for Sheffielders out to northern parts of the city.

As my grandparents were amongst those who lived in Corporation Buildings, I spent a lot of my childhood days and young adult life in the vicinity. In fact, for most of our family, Snig Hill became almost the centre of the Universe!

As a small boy I can remember Saturday mornings at the bottom, where there used to be a bit of open ground, where I watched with intrigue an escapologist as he mysteriously managed to escape from a sack he'd been tied and chained-up in.

Another memory was watching one or two unfortunate cyclists who would get their wheels stuck in the tram-line and have to follow it down the hill until they could get out... sometimes falling off!

Another thing that brings a smile is the Red Circle Library on Snig Hill where some of the bookshelves were in the windows. Mischievously, me and my pal, David Finn, would shut his dog in the window, causing a definite break in the library's customary silence!

For those who lived in Snig Hill, all the city centre shops and the Market were, of course, most convenient as Alan recalled: "Oh yes, they were and my mother would go round to the Market in her carpet-slippers!"

The old Black Swan had of course become more widely and affectionately known as 'The Mucky Duck' and continued to feature live entertainment with weekly piano sing-alongs. For the cooler music fan, Club-Basie operated in one of the remaining upstairs rooms of the pub and presented weekly sessions for modern jazz enthusiasts, featuring ensembles such as The Savoy Quintet providing the live music.

For another bunch of cool cats, one of the shops in the 1950s below The Black Swan was Winston's which would be frequented by all the young fashion-conscious guys and gals and the shop was probably the main supplier of outfits for Teddy-boys and Teddy-girls. Many will remember those garish, brightly coloured drape jackets and drainpipe trousers for both him and her plus other accessories displayed in the window.

As Jenny Colley recalls: "My brother bought a sparkly black jacket from there in the late 50s having seen Lonnie Donegan in one at the City Hall. Needless to say, he never wore it. It just came home and hung in the wardrobe!"

As I much preferred the music of the era rather than the fashion, Haroll's electrical shop up across the street was where I'd

The centre of the Universe? Well, perhaps not, but John Firminger recalls that Snig Hill was once a big attraction for fans of piano sing-alongs, Teddy Boy fashions and even escapologists... and it was a place for cyclists to avoid

sometimes spend half-an-hour or so gazing at their display of some of the latest LPs, whilst just a few yards away a hot chestnut man was always a welcome sight.

Jenny recalls another purchase from a shop in Snig Hill: "I got my first tape-recorder from Wigfalls at about 2/3d a week for about two years! It taught me never to get anything 'on tic' ever again!"

With the re-development in the 60s, The Black Swan enjoyed a spectacular re-birth when it presented live entertainment again. Throughout a ten-year period, Sheffielders enjoyed many nights of live music under the auspices of jovial and friendly host Terry Steeples. So many great bands performed there with perhaps the most memorable night being when Joe Cocker appeared there the same date as he hit number one on the charts with 'With A Little Help From My Friends'. Other 'Mucky Duck' faves included dynamic soul show-band O'Hara's Playboys, horror-rockers Light Fantastic, prog rock combo Patto and Sheffield's other favourite musical sons, Bitter Suite. Billy Fury and The Ronettes also appeared there.

At the time, the building actually housed three hostelries with, underneath The Black Swan, The Merry England Bar and just a few yards further down was the smaller Brewery Tap which became my Grandma's local. Another place my Gran would gravitate to on a daily basis was Thorpe's the bookies whose large betting shop was situated on the floor above The Black Swan. In the older building next to The Black Swan was the small upstairs office where two of The Black Swan's popular disc-jockeys-turned-agents, Pat Reid and Ray Stuart, kept some of the local bands working with their PR Promotions agency.

Also adding to the activity was the ABC Cinema on the bottom corner of Angel Street where if you didn't go in to see a film you could while away an hour making a coffee last in the Concourse lounge.

In recent times some of the area's tradition for live music has being upheld admirably by The Boardwalk. Located in the same building as The Black Swan and having previously being called the curiously named The Compleat Angler and the more familiar Mucky Duck, the venue became recognised as a major live music venue both locally and nationally. Since it opened in 1997, amongst those who have appeared there are Robert Plant, Jools Holland, Paul Carrack, BR549, Gary Barlowe, James Burton, Screaming Lord Sutch, Wilko Johnson and Charlie Chuck, a varied and impressive list indeed.

At present The Boardwalk appears to be closed, hopefully temporarily, whilst downstairs, Under The Boardwalk is getting ready to reopen, reviving the name of The Black Swan Bar again with its familiar sign looking down once more from the top of the building.

Across the road, shops and a café have opened up and the refurbished Corporation Buildings, now designated as City Lodgings will hopefully soon see people taking up residency. All this activity is certainly a return to some semblance of how things used to be on Snig Hill.

Otherwise, for many other people, Snig Hill is simply the place to wait for a bus. Unfortunately, this last observation seems to have contributed towards an ongoing problem with litter around the top of Snig Hill. It is discarded near the entrance to the Boardwalk, probably by the people waiting for buses. It goes without saying that people should of course have a little more consideration for their home town and make their own contribution towards the resurgence of one of the once liveliest streets in town.

• Do you have any special personal memories of a particular place in Sheffield? Why not share them with other readers of this publication? Write to My Kind of Town, 24 Hutcliffe Wood Road, Beauchief, Sheffield, S8 0EX, or email mike@heronpublications.co.uk

Images of old Snig Hill and (above) how this corner of the city centre looks today

The former Norfolk Street premises of Radio Sheffield where all manner of celebrity guests called in on Saturday mornings

The odd couple

Mike Firth recalls Saturday mornings spent at Norfolk Street in the company of a Methodist Minister and the artist formerly known as Frankenstein

HANDS up anyone who recalls Michael Cooke and Ray Stuart presenting 'Downtown Saturday' on Radio Sheffield.

The show transformed my life at the back end of 1972 when I phoned in to enter a competition and won myself £18 worth of new records. A large bundle of vinyl arrived in the post a few days later but there was one slight problem: I didn't have a record player.

Following a trip to Woolies to buy a red and white plastic-coated Dansette (with volume and tone buttons, plus auto-change), I went on to torture mum and dad with Wizzard's 'Ball Park Incident' throughout the Christmas holiday. Then I discovered Slade.

But back to 'Downtown Saturday'. Reflecting on the show, it was years ahead of its time, being broadcast with special guests and an audience live from Radio Sheffield's city centre Norfolk Street 'Information Centre'. The station's main studio in those days was at Westbourne Road.

Local preacher Michael Cooke - who later went on to be a presenter on Look North - and Sheffield singer Ray Stuart - frontman with local band Frankenstein and The Monsters

Michael Cooke

- were an odd couple to put in charge of such a show. Even stranger was their eclectic mix of special guests.

Big name cabaret entertainers who were in the area performing at The Fiesta and The Aquarius were given an early morning invitation to be there and you were never quite sure who would be entertaining in the 'studio' which was basically a large shop front.

A new band called Mud were there when I first visited Downtown Saturday, most likely having been supporting another band at the City Hall the previous evening.

Acker Bilk called in at Norfolk Street one week, The Four Tops the next and then Gene Pitney, The Scaffold, Ronnie Hilton and Frankie Vaughan.

Some of the nation's biggest stars at the time were comics who appeared on Granada TV's hugely popular Saturday evening show 'The Comedians' and Ken Goodwin, Duggie Brown, Frank Carson and Charlie Williams were frequent guests at Downtown Saturday.

It was an autograph-hunter's paradise, although I missed out on the signature of the biggest star of all - and I blame Frank Carson for that. The comic caused total uproar in the studio, diverting all the attention away from another much quieter guest sitting patiently in the corner, waiting to be interviewed. No-one took much notice of the young guy with the dreadlocks - Bob Marley.

I still have 'Ball Park Incident' and most of the other records I won from 'Downtown Saturday', minus a Donovan LP and a few obscure albums which were immediately despatched to Violet May's "buying and selling" record shop.

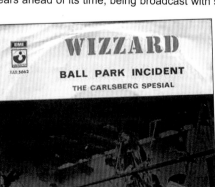

Frank Carson

10

Living in a box

John Firminger's parents on the Prefabricated Arbourthorne Estate In 1955

Built in a single day, Prefabs were erected after the war, designed to last for a decade-or-so until more substantial housing could be provided. So why are some Sheffield folk still proud to call them home more than 60 years later? John Firminger grew up in a city Prefab and he reports that the buildings were far from basic, offering some mod cons many other Sheffielders could only dream about

ALTHOUGH there is only a mere fraction still around of all those that were built at the end of the war, the small number of Prefabricated Houses - Prefabs - still standing in Sheffield serve as a reminder to many of us of our early family life.

Prefabs, the "temporary" homes built after World War II were meant to last ten years but some have been around for six decades.

Built in 1948, Prefabricated Houses were originally erected as a temporary stop-gap to provide homes for those who'd lost theirs in The Blitz.

Looking like bungalows, groups of Prefabs could be quickly erected in just a single day - often by POWs - and they were located in various suburbs of the city, wherever there was enough open land to accommodate them. They originally had a short life expectancy and people moved into them probably until new, more formidable replacement housing could be provided.

Not all Prefabs were of the same design; some had their front doors in the middle whilst others had them at the side with steps leading up to them, depending on where they were built. Some had flat roofs and some were sloping.

Inside they were all pretty roomy and, above all, practical. For those who lived in these dwellings, it certainly represented a new way of life as many people had come from some of the grimy back-to-back streets of the inner-city areas.

In addition to being practical,

they were quite futuristic too, including features that were new to many Sheffield homes at the time.

Sybil O'Brien remembers the Prefab she lived in, at Scraith Wood Drive, Shirecliffe: "We had a bathroom and an inside toilet. The kitchen was fully equipped with a modern electric cooker and a built-in fridge now known, I suppose, as 'integrated'. The cupboards were all built in including a large pantry. It was heaven for my mum to have loads of workspace to do her baking."

Within its cosy confines, the one this writer lived in was on Errington Road, Arbourthorne (now Berners Road). It consisted of two bedrooms, a living room with small coal fire, small doors with perspex windows and kitchen. The front door on the left-hand side of the building led into the hallway in which my dad kept his tropical fish and also where we also had the luxury of an inside toilet and bathroom. The cupboard space included a lovely warm airing cupboard into which we could climb when we were just little kids!

Another practical space-saving idea was a table that folded back into the wall in the kitchen. Although compact, looking back, they seemed quite spacious with certainly plenty of room for me, my mum, dad and brother. The small electric fridge certainly helped to make me very popular with my pals in summer when my mum would make up a tray of ice-lollies. The surrounding pavements were often

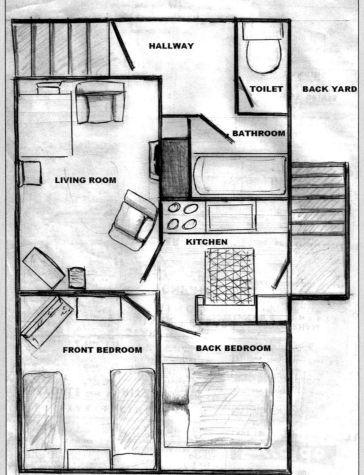

A diagram of the type of Prefab which was home to John Firminger and his family

Some Prefabs were clearly built to last as these cosy bungalows in Eckington and Killamarsh demonstrate

flag-stones which lined the cemented roadways.

Sybil O'Brien recalls how her Prefab was set-out: "From the kitchen there was a door into the living room; this was big enough to hold a very old oak table and chairs and another sideboard, plus a three-piece suite, the TV and the radiogram. At the end of the hall was the toilet and separate bathroom and to the left two bedrooms.

"I had to share with my brother Bill until he got to an age where it was not appropriate and then I went in with my mum and dad. No wonder I never had a little brother or sister!

"The bedrooms all had built-in wardrobes and huge cupboards, big enough to hold lots of toys and, as I got older, an illicit copy of Fanny Hill hidden behind my world wildlife magazines. Yes, my mum did find it but blamed Bill who had moved out, joining the Merchant Navy in the early 60s and so I had at last my own room.

"In the back yard, corrugated 'Anderson Shelter-like' coal-houses stood which would also be used for keeping our bikes in.

"We all had coal fires and therefore a coal house; this was a 'wriggly tin' construction in the garden, big enough for coal but also a great storage area once dad had erected shelves."

Some prefabs stood only for around their designated life-span, but this was more by bad luck than planning. In 1962, Sheffield was hit by gales and a number of Prefabs in various locations were blown down 'like a pack of cards' as one eye-witness described. For those who'd lost their homes, refuge was provided for dwellers on the Arbourthorne in nearby Norfolk Secondary Modern and Hurlfield

Surrounded by well kept gardens, these Prefabs have stood at Lea Road, Loxley, for more then 60 years

schools.

Strangely enough, although the Prefab I lived in stood on a high, windy corner, it remained standing through the high winds of previous years but maybe that was something to do with my mum getting up in the middle of the night and holding onto the bedroom walls!

Mounted on bricks with a concrete foundation, they were made from sheets of asbestos fixed together, and despite the asbestosis scare of the 1980s, I can't recall anybody who lived in the Prefabs ever coming to any harm. On the contrary, they provided shelter and protection and proof probably lies within the number of Prefabs still standing and still inhabited.

A recent article on Prefabs in the Daily Mail incorrectly cited an estate of them in Catford, London, as the only remaining one of its kind in England. Reminders of them are also still huddled together in a handful of locations around Sheffield. These include small estates in Killamarsh, Ecclesfield and Eckington.

In retrospect, many of those who lived in them look back at them with great affection, whilst those who still call them home obviously regard them with pride.

Whether enjoying a reinvention or simply a long, yet modest life, their preservation has allowed Prefabs to maintain their practicality and attraction far beyond their years, reiterating their original claim 'Prefabs are for people'.

• Did you live in a Prefab? What was it like? Send your recollections to My Kind of Town.

CAN you recall where Sheffield's Prefabs were located?

John Firminger remembers the following locations in and around the city:

Errington Road, Errington Avenue, Errington Crescent, Northern Avenue and Eastern Avenue at Arbourthorne.

East Bank Road and Madehurst Road.

Beighton, Killamarsh and Eckington.

Herries Road in Sheffield.

Mill Road at Ecclesfield.

Richmond Park Crescent at Handsworth.

Mansfield Road at Intake.

Lee Road at Loxley.

Ridgeway Road at Manor Top.

Bernard Street at Park.

Holgate Road at Parson Cross.

Penrith Road at Shirecliffe.

Skye Edge.

Green Oak at Totley.

Wensley Street at Wincobank.

Can you remember any others?

Welcome to our 1970s attractions

Reading up on Sheffield's visitor attractions from the early 1970s, Mike Firth discovers we were a city proud of our new developments, markets, department stores, clean air... and show-jumping

THE people charged with promoting Sheffield in the 1970s didn't spend all their budget on the 'City on the Move' film. They brought out fascinating little publications too, including 'Sheffield Visitor', a slimline guide which offers an insight into just how rapidly the city was developing.

Of particular interest in this particular 1974 booklet are the many attractions, relatively new and exciting at the time, which have now long since disappeared.

The 'Wedding Cake' was there; did you know it was Britain's first purpose-built register office? The colourful booklet commented that Millhouses Park had "a very exciting Lido to satisfy family requirements" and that the new Castle Square development - soon to be dubbed the 'Hole in the Road' - was "unusual in design and concept and well worth a visit". For the active visitor to Sheffield, the new Sheaf Valley Baths offered "sophisticated amenities" right in the city centre.

Produced by Sheffield City Promotion Committee, the publication informed visitors that they could expect to be surprised by what they discovered: "The environment is entirely different from yesteryear. This is largely due to the city's clean air programme which has made Sheffield virtually smokeless and probably the cleanest industrial city in Europe."

The post-war building programme had, readers were told, "given full rein to architectural ingenuity which, taking advantage of the hills on which Sheffield stands, produced dramatic visual effects".

The publication's 'Welcome' article went on to say that the complete redevelopment of the city centre had brought with it a new concept in traffic and pedestrian control. New shops and office blocks had replaced many pre-war buildings and most of the civic buildings had been cleaned: "Mature trees have been planted and flower gardens introduced, providing a bright, clean, environment in all the main thoroughfares."

So how should 1974 visitors to Sheffield have made the most of their stay in the city? Well, following their trip to enjoy the new "vehicular roundabout, pedestrian underpass and subterranean shopping precinct" in Castle Square, they could visit one of the city's six department stores - more than any other city north of London. An unusual aspect of shopping in Sheffield was that "many of the larger stores tend to have not one, but two outlets in the main shopping centre due to its long, linear, layout."

The Moor and Haymarket/Waingate were popular places in which to shop, plus Fargate - featured on the publication's cover - which was "a particularly pleasant shopping area, being completely pedestrianised". The virtues of the Castle and Sheaf Markets were also trumpeted to visitors.

The relatively new Crucible Theatre was a big attraction (The Lyceum was closed to drama in those days) and the City Hall staged weekly symphony concerts as well as "light entertainment" including shows, pop concerts and wrestling. For late night entertainment, two of Europe's largest clubs could be found in the city centre - Bailey's and The Fiesta.

For movie fans, this really was the place to be and Sheffield Visitor reports that "the major cinema chains have adopted a 'two in one' system at the two principal venues. A complex of three small cinemas is also conveniently located at the side of the Grosvenor House Hotel in Charter Square."

In the world of sport, tourists were told of Sheffield's proud heritage in football, fishing and bowls and that golfers were also well catered for. Athletes had a "full-scale athletics arena, equipped to full Amateur Athletics Association standards", in Hillsborough Park. Surprisingly, equestrianism was also booming: "Sheffield is fast building a reputation as the show-jumping centre of the north with regular meetings throughout the summer."

Oh to be a visitor to Sheffield in the 1970s!

An orchestra entertains at the City Hall (left) and the audience at The Fiesta (right) enjoy a Jack Jones performance to accompany their chicken in a basket meals

Sheffield Visitor

Three images of fabulous Fargate from the Sheffield Visitor publication: The Goodwin Fountain (above), the top of Chapel Walk (left) and people enjoying the city's new pedestrianised areas (right)

Selling my pages from history

We've all seen scenes from auction rooms on TV, but have you ever wondered just what it is like to see your own item go under the hammer? Mike Firth now knows after selling a rare Sheffield United football programme

SEVENTY-five years ago, tens of thousands of Sheffielders boarded London-bound steam trains to see if their United team could upset hot favourites Arsenal in the 14th final of the FA Cup to be played at Wembley.

A single Ted Drake goal won the Cup for the Gunners and as dejected Unitedites returned north, one of them was unwittingly doing me quite a favour. Tucked away inside his overcoat pocket was a red, white and blue programme from the game, a sixpenny souvenir of a big day out which the supporter probably kept for the rest of his life.

Almost 40 years later the programme turned up in the window of a second-hand shop in Woodseats - Shelton's at the bottom of Aisthorpe Road - and a passing schoolboy recognised it as a rarity. After all, 1936 was the last time the Blades had reached an FA Cup final. Sadly, that is still the case.

The boy popped inside, parted with a large slice of his week's spending money and proudly walked home with a piece of football history in his pocket.

I was that schoolboy and although I possessed a collection of hundreds of football programmes - all kept in suitcases in alphabetical order - I recognised that this particular publication was something rather special; it was an investment.

For almost 35 years this souvenir remained the pride and joy of my collection and I often recalled the day I bought it in exchange for one of those new, strangely-shaped 50 pence decimal coins. Each time I looked at it I wondered how much its value might have increased and whether my investment had been a wise one.

I was to find out when I chatted to Robert Lea, a football souvenir expert who mixes his passion for sporting antiquities with working at Sheffield Auction Gallery. Robert, from Barnsley, has been in the auction business since 1979, working for the Sheffield-based company for the past ten years.

Taking a look at my programme from 1936, his eyes immediately lit up.

"It's in good condition and the staples are not rusty," he detected. "There is nothing written on it and apart from a small scuff mark on the cover there are no marks, blemishes or punched holes. Anything like that can considerably detract

from the value but some are still desirable even if they are slightly grubby or torn."

Being almost 75 years old, this item was indeed something of a rarity, with Robert having auctioned only a dozen-or-so copies in the past decade.

The mid-1930s was clearly a fabulous time for Sheffield football. Wednesday beat West Bromwich Albion to win the FA Cup in 1935 and, according to Robert, surviving programmes from that match are mostly in a similar condition.

"It rained that day and spectators folded their programmes in two and slipped them into their pockets to keep them dry; that's why most of the ones we see have a crease down the centre."

So just how much did Robert estimate my own Cup Final souvenir from 1936 could be worth?

Sheffield United captain Harry Hooper and Arsenal's Alex James shake hands before the 1936 FA Cup Final

"It might fetch £300 and if you want to include it in one of our specialist football programme and sporting memorabilia auctions you should be looking at a reserved price of £200," he advised me.

With the auction date fast approaching, I had to make up my mind whether it was time to part with the pride and joy of my collection. For a potential £200-plus earning, it surely was and I handed the programme to Robert in exchange for a pink auction receipt.

More than 60 collectors and dealers were in attendance at the company's next Football Programmes and Sporting Memorabilia Auction and, picking up a catalogue, I noticed that my item was listed as Lot 155 of 522 items. Looking around at the gathering, these were, like myself, enthusiasts who had been collecting programmes since their school days. Which one of them might be walking home with Lot 155, I wondered?

Robert, now with gavel in hand, conducted the day's business with haste and all manner of programmes, books and unusual souvenirs were attracting bids. None, however, had reached £100, let alone £200, so I was beginning to wonder if I might be taking home the programme myself.

The moment of truth had arrived and Robert informed the gathering that there had been much interest in Lot 155, the 1936 FA Cup Final programme. He invited an opening bid of £260 and, before I could even think about holding my breath, he went on, "two eighty... three hundred..."

The closing bid was an astonishing £360 and as I scanned the

Robert Lea of ELR Auctions inspects Mike's 1936
FA Cup Final programme prior to the sale

saleroom to spot the purchaser, Robert announced that it had
been bought by a bidder on the internet. I later found out that the
programme's new owner was from Lancashire.

Reaching the car with a smile on my face, I couldn't help
recalling Del's comment to Rodney in their three-wheeler van
parked outside Sotheby's: "Well, we've had worse days."

Even allowing for commission, lot fee and insurance deduction,
my 50p investment as a schoolboy had indeed proved a wise one.
How would I spend my earnings? Perhaps my wife and daughter
will write an article about that.

And although my programme has now gone, in its place I
have auction sale catalogue with my item listed as Lot 155.
I'm going to save it; you never know, one day it might be worth
something.

• *Sheffield Auction Gallery stages regular specialist sales at
their premises at Windsor Road, Meersbrook, Sheffield, S8 8UB.
They also have a diary of valuation days. Go to:
www.sheffieldauctiongallery.com or telephone 0114 281 6161.
You can visit the saleroom for advice on all aspects of sale
and valuation.*

The Arsenal versus Sheffield United programme
cost sixpence and included advertisements for
Mazda lightbulbs, Lanson Champagne,
Watney's beer, Ecko radio sets, Seager's egg flip
and, of course, Bovril.

Teams for the big match at Wembley were:
Arsenal; Wilson, Male, Hapgood, Crayston,
Roberts, Copping, Hulme, Bowden, Drake,
James, Bastin.

Sheffield United; Smith, Hooper, Wilkinson,
Jackson, Johnson, McPherson, Barton, Barclay,
Dodds, Pickering, Williams.

HILLSBOROUGH, SHEFFIELD
FLOODLIGHT MATCH
COMBINED
SHEFFIELD XI.
v
INTERNATIONAL
XI.

Wednesday, 9th March
Kick-off 7.30 p.m.

Reserved Seat
5/-

Gangway 1
ROW A
SEAT 50

Secretary and Manager

Dooley's big night

It cost five bob for a seat in the stand and sixpence for a programme for one of the city's greatest nights of football

My Kind of Hero

OFFICIAL SOUVENIR, SIXPENCE

DEREK DOOLEY
TRUST FUND

Floodlight Match

WEDNESDAY, 9th MARCH, 1955, Kick-off 7.30 p.m.

SHEFFIELD XI.
V.
INTERNATIONAL XI.

WHEN you consider sporting legends, no-one ranks higher in the esteem of local folk than the late Derek Dooley and the two items on this page are souvenirs of one of the city's greatest footballing events.

After the bustling, flame-haired centre-forward lost a leg following a Sheffield Wednesday game at Preston North End on February 14th, 1953, the people of Sheffield rallied to support him.

A testimonial match was played at Hillsborough between a Sheffield XI and a team of internationals. The game was attended by 55,000 supporters and raised £7,500. Another £2,700 was donated to a fund for Dooley by local newspapers and £15,000 by a shilling fund held in the city.

Dooley, who grew up at Pitsmoor, scored 62 goals in 60 games and in all grades of football for Wednesday he bagged 180 goals in just 166 matches.

The star-studded fund-raising game for Dooley on March 9th, 1955, was the first fixture to be played under floodlights at Hillsborough. It featured a combined Wednesday and United team and the opposition included legends such as John Charles, Alex Forbes, Stanley Matthews and Tommy Lawton.

• Can anyone from your family recall attending this match? We would be delighted to hear their recollections.

Flashbck to 1966 and a glimpse of how the Hillbilly Cats looked in their early years

Cool for Cats

They've been entertaining Sheffield music fans for more than 45 years and John Firminger reports that The Hillbilly Cats continue to play only the kind of music they want to

HAVING been active since the mid-1960s, The Hillbilly Cats can rightly boast themselves to be Sheffield's longest surviving working group. However, such a statistic is something that remaining founder members, Pete Jackson and Graham 'Satch' Sargent, acknowledge with modest pride.

Also, despite the years mounting up and the various musical preferences of the world around them, the band maintains its original intentions and proudly sticks basically to the same kind of music they've always set out to play.

The band's origins go back to Sheffield rock'n'beat combos, Dean Marshall & The Deputies followed by The Lizards. Two of the band's members, brothers Roger and Pete Jackson, decided to break away from the competitiveness of the local pop scene and return to the music they loved which was the sounds of early Elvis, Carl Perkins and The Everly Brothers. After meeting up with two other like-minded musicians, singer Graham 'Satch' Sargent and guitarist Dave 'Dia' Jones from the Dave Graham Four, they got together as a four-piece to put their mutual musical ideas into practice.

At the time, there was an under-current of bands playing some of the vintage sounds like Chuck Fowler, Scott William, Steve Denton

and Frank White. However, these outfits also made certain compromises and included more contemporary material in order to acquire regular bookings. The Hillbilly Cats, on the other hand, made no such concessions and gave a full commitment to their musical choices from the outset, playing rockabilly and country.

With Pete on bass and vocals, 'Satch' on guitar and vocals, Roger on drums and vocals and 'Dia' on lead guitar, the band was initially called The Rockin' Billies. This had been given to them by agent Pat Reid and derived from a nickname, common amongst the rock 'n' roll fraternity. Adding a further touch of authenticity and inspired, of course, by Elvis' original bass-man Bill Black, Pete Jackson went out and bought a double bass from Barratt's, the large music store in Manchester.

The combo played their first gig on February 5th at one of the regular out-of-town band gigs, The Lathkil Hotel, near Bakewell. After a couple of bookings the band changed their name to The Hillbilly Cats which had been one of the early names given to Elvis and personified the band's musical outlook.

With a definite 'play what we want' policy, the band's repertoire included classic songs from the likes of Elvis, Carl Perkins, The Everlys, Johnny Cash and Jerry Lee Lewis. Sticking to their musical guns, it wasn't long before they discovered a lot more people also wanted to hear what they had to offer. As a result, the band began to build up a steady following around the city pubs from as far as Frecheville to High Green.

Not long after they'd established themselves, drummer Roger Jackson got the call to join Dave Berry's Cruisers and Chesterfield drummer Johnny Pearson became a Hillbilly Cat for a while. Another worthy addition to the Cats line-up came when steel-guitarist Brian 'Larney' Terry joined the band. Another instrument uncommon on the local scene at the time, it helped the band to

My Kind of Band

fulfill their intention to incorporate some excellent country material into their set. This would bring in songs from more favourite artists like Buck Owens, Hank Thompson, George Jones and, of course, Hank Williams.

New Year's Eve 1965 saw the HBC's join forces with fellow rockers Dave Hawley and Chuck Fowler and their respective bands to stage a Rock 'n' Country Jamboree at the Highcliffe Hotel (now The Greystones). The event played to a packed house and clearly confirmed the interest in the emerging rockabilly movement within the city.

Taking their music further afield, in May 1967 the HBC's performed an impressive set in London at the prestigious Folk Voice Concert for which the boys won acclaim from both the audience and press alike for their efforts.

Following Johnny Pearson's departure, the Cats took on young drummer Phil Allen from local mod group The Square Circles. Not totally conversant with the Cats' musical preferences, he filled in for just a few gigs before ex-Cruiser and equally devout rockabilly fan John Riley provided the group with more authoritative drumming and also additional vocals.

There were a few gaps in the band's continuity through the years as members kept active working with other musicians. These would be with such performers as Johnny Tempest, Pat Leslie, Radio 4, The Rock 'n' Roll Road Show and Rollin' Back. However, throughout these periods there would always be some evidence of the Hillbilly Cats' music in these diversions.

The early 1980s saw The Hillbilly Cats back together and rockin' just as good as ever and the band was invited to perform at the annual Northern Buddy Holly Tribute at the Royal Victoria Hotel. In the line-up at this time was talented guitarist Dave Sanderson whose Chet Atkins-inspired playing gave the band's sound some additional quality. Back together on a fairly regular basis, the band set up a Friday night residency, attracting followers out to the Loxely Golf Club, Bradfield. During their stint at the venue, guitarist and singer Joe Beckett would become a regular and valid member.

In the 1990s the band moved nearer town and took up another residency at the Upperthorpe Hotel where they enjoyed a full house every first Friday of the month. Always eager to play with the band, veteran guitarist Dave Hopper had now joined and added his expertise to the band's musical format.

In recognition of their longevity and musical commitment, their monthly gig would attract a number of other musicians who'd come along to either enjoy the music or get up as invited guests. One of these was Sheffield's rock 'n' blues legend Frank White who was subsequently invited to join the band for their monthly residency and created further interest in their activities.

Another regular guest is young pianist Dale Storr whose leanings towards the music of New Orleans added another dimension to the Cats' musical format. Following in his dad's footsteps, Richard Hawley also has naturally a strong affinity with the Cats and also enjoys sitting in with them whenever he gets the chance, as do some of the city's other second generation rockers.

Over the years the Hillbilly Cats rallied round to take part in various charity events in aid of some of their fellow musicians who have suffered ill-health or are no longer with us. Staged at either the Park & Arbourthorne or St Philip's Social Clubs, both now sadly long-gone venues, the band always made a special effort for the occasion by bringing in former members like guitarists 'Dia' Jones and Bryn Jones and special guest Dave Hawley.

Sadly their own member, Joe Beckett passed away in 2001, but his role with the Cats will remain a cherished one in the memories of both the band and their followers. Joe was also responsible for taking the time to record performances and make some of the band's music available on CD, serving as a permanent record.

The summer of 2004 saw the Hillbilly Cats' original line-up reform for another special occasion. This was a one-off revival of The Sun Sound Club, the gig held in the 1960s where all the city's rockabilly bands found an appreciative audience under the auspices of rockin' DJ, Gaspin' Gus. For the gig, original guitarist Dave 'Dia' Jones and drummer Roger Jackson were back in action together with Pete Jackson and 'Satch' Sargent and they sounded as good as always.

A 2005 line-up of The Hillbilly Cats

Whilst featuring this occasional original line-up, Roger Jackson and John Riley have at different times seemingly alternated drumming duties as members of the Hillbilly Cats. When Roger eventually relinquished his role with the Cats last year, John took over permanently. Occasional Frank White also shares the lead guitar slot with Dave Hopper.

They are now in residence every first Friday of the month at The Office, Upperthorpe, a most conducive venue where the band continue to keep audiences musically satisfied and entertained. Still featuring a range of vintage classics by early Elvis, Eddie Cochran, Johnny Cash, Everly Brothers, Chuck Berry and Carl Perkins along with one or two more contemporary songs from The Eagles, Don McClean and Dobie Gray, the Cats are pretty much as they always have been.

Playing the music with the same conviction whilst interspersing it with the band's usual humorous banter, has been the reason for the continuous loyalty they enjoy and, over 46 years on, long may they keep rockin'.

Who were your favourite local performers?

Which Sheffield area bands do you have fond memories of? Who were the local musicians who entertained you in the 1950s, 60s and 70s and which venues did you go attend to see them perform? Did you play in a band yourself?

Share your memories and old pictures with other readers by sending them to us here at My Kind of Town, 24 Hutcliffe Wood Road, Beauchief, Sheffield, S8 0EX, or mike@heronpublications.co.uk

H E'S taken to the stage with Sadler's Wells Royal Ballet and 'directed' the Royal Shakespeare Company, but for thousands of Sheffielders Gerry Kersey is known as the city's voice of nostalgia.

If anyone wishes to monitor the popularity of his Monday evening Radio Sheffield programme, they should simply speak to the station's switchboard operator whenever Gerry's show is cancelled due to commentary of a rescheduled football match.

"My regular listeners are absolutely steeped in it and they are very loyal," says Gerry. "What has amazed me is the scale of the response I get from people; they are devoted to the programme and get very cross when it is occasionally postponed to make way for football."

Now well into his fifth decade as a local radio broadcaster, Gerry recalls his early days with Radio Sheffield with much fondness. Working alongside presenters including June Hurst and education broadcaster Dave Sheasby, one of his first roles was simply to come up with sound effects and background noises - but he was soon hooked on radio.

"They invented a character for me, Frank Forthright, who was rather an opinionated person," recalls Gerry. "We recorded various comments from him and played them at schools to get opinions and responses from children.

"That was the first moment I thought I really wanted to get involved in radio full time."

With Radio Sheffield in those days based at leafy Westbourne Road, one of Gerry's other tasks was to review local plays for an 'On Stage' programme, presented by Mavis Carter. In the early 70s he took over producing the show and it became his programme.

Educated at Firth Park Grammar School, Gerry had served for two years with the RAF at Bridgnorth. He worked in advertising and publicity for a holiday company and also for Stanley Tools but decided to quit his job to concentrate on radio full time.

"I just decided the time was right to take my chance," he says.

To begin with, he did stand-in work when other presenters were absent and also recorded many "voice-overs" for the station.

In 1973/74 Gerry found himself immersed in nostalgia for the first time, researching and presenting a series exploring the history of theatre in Sheffield, called 'Early Doors One And Six'. The task was a challenging and exhausting one, with Gerry often working into the early hours of the morning.

"I became totally engrossed in the nostalgia of it all, working very, very long hours and the project was quite shattering," he says. "The programmes were a reasonable archive of Sheffield theatres, dating back to Queen Anne's time. Theatres have always been an important part of local life here in Sheffield and in the 1890s there were eight or nine in the West Bars area."

22

Mister Nostalgia

No publication looking at bygone days in Sheffield would be quite complete without mention of local radio stalwart Gerry Kersey (pictured left), the man who makes Monday nights the most enjoyable evening of the week for thousands of local people. Mike Firth calls in at Radio Sheffield to meet him

Proud of his work, Gerry retained some tapes of the shows and also presented copies to a local history society.

With commercial radio arriving on the local scene, Gerry left the BBC in 1980 to work for Radio Hallam, teaming up with broadcasting legends such as Roger Moffatt and Bill Crozier.

"Roger was a real legend with a radio voice to die for and I took over his programme in the mid-1980s."

Bill had presented 'Two-Way Family Favourites' nationally for many years so Gerry was also honoured to succeed him on Hallam's request show, playing listeners' favourite records five nights a week plus Sunday lunchtimes.

"It was a fairly solid piece of broadcasting to do," he recalls.

Going on to enjoy a 17-year career in commercial radio with Hallam, Great Yorkshire Radio, Classic Gold and Great Yorkshire Gold, Gerry recalls there were some wonderful highlights: "I was asked to do so many things and at one point was doing 11 shows a week."

Having presented a twice-weekly oldies show on Great Yorkshire Gold, nostalgia continued to be his forte after returning to Radio Sheffield in 1997.

Now he is a much-respected stalwart of the station and his three-hour Monday evening show is enjoyed by thousands of people across South Yorkshire, plus countless exiles who tune in around the world via the internet. One of the weekly highlights is Gerry's weekly 'Memory Test' - quizzes are still frowned upon at the BBC!

The programme originally featured memories and music from the 1940s up to the1960s but at beginning of the new decade in 2010 there was a conscious decision to move on and cover more recent times.

Says Gerry: "I live for now and I live for today. I don't live in the past but I have a huge love for some things which have gone by. Once when I began to question why I so enjoy working on radio, I realised it dated back to me growing up in Bellhouse Road at Shiregreen, listening to 'Much Binding in the Marsh' and 'Have a Go' on the radio. I still love listening to them these days, even though they are hopelessly dated and younger people find no interest in them whatsoever.

"I was also taken to the Empire Theatre to see variety and that had a huge impact on me.

"There is a tremendous comfort and safety in the past because it has happened. It can't be changed and it can't hurt you any more.

"I think that's why people enjoy talking about many of the things which have happened in their lives; things which we discuss on Monday evenings."

Gerry's BBC career has been punctuated by "little insurgencies into Radio 2" where he was once the northern correspondent for 'Around Midnight' with Brian Matthew.

On one occasion, Gerry taped an interview with the widow of Georgi Markov, the novelist and playwright who had defected from Bulgaria in 1969. There was national and international interest in a play of his at The Crucible Studio and Gerry's fascinating interview was broadcast around the world, including parts of the Eastern Bloc.

Gerry's career has seen him carry out all manner of memorable challenges including taking the controls of an aircraft and driving a double-decker bus... but how did his impressive connections with top flight ballet and the RSC come about?

"When the Sadler's Wells Royal Ballet came to Sheffield to perform in a big top in Norfolk Park, I found myself heavily involved in assisting them with their publicity and, in particular, I helped them find a number of local 'extras' to appear in their performances.

"As a thank you they wanted to give me tickets but I already had some. When they asked if there was anything else they could do to show their gratitude, I asked if I could appear myself as an extra in one of the ballets. So that's how I came to do three nights in 'Giselle' with the Sadler's Wells Royal Ballet. I had a wonderful costume and it was a fabulous experience."

With tongue firmly in his cheek, Gerry goes on to explain how he came to direct the RSC...

"They were doing some appearances around the provinces and were at the Hurlfield Campus in Sheffield, performing for students and then the general public.

"I was there for Radio Sheffield, interviewing Sir Ian McKellen, and when I was told they all wanted a meal and could I recommend a good Italian restaurant, I 'directed' them from Hurlfield to a place I knew at Ecclesall Road!"

Left: A big smile from Gerry Kersey for this 1950 school photograph at Firth Park Grammar

Below: Gerry's National Service days were spent at RAF Bridgnorth. Can you spot him? He's fifth from the left on the centre row

On the buses

If you caught the Circular bus you could be gone for the best part of a day. Mike Firth inspects an old timetable

S HEFFIELD folk have always been proud of their transport systems. The city's tramcars were famous throughout the land and local folk knew they could rely on them, whatever the weather, in days of peace and war, to get them to where they needed to be.

Since they disappeared in 1960, we have had all manner of other ways of getting around. Buses have been plodding up and down our seven hills and through the city centre for generations; we've had rear-entrance buses, front-entrance buses, double-deckers, single deckers, the City Clipper (does anyone remember the City Clopper?) and even a bendy bus. Now, of course, we also have Supertram. We've had bus lanes, bus gates, bus stations and a Transport Interchange which people of a certain age still refer to as "Pond Street".

One of the biggest eras of change arrived in the early 1970s when bus conductors began to be phased out, leaving the driver to take passengers' fares.

There was the old joke about a double-decker crashing one day and when the driver was quizzed about what had happened, he replied: "I don't know, I was upstairs collecting fares at the time."

Thousands of Sheffield folk - my grandad included - used to subscribe to Sheffield Transport's chunky Bus and Rail Timetable which, I seem to recall, was published a couple of times each year. It included routes, destinations, service numbers, times, details of special early-morning and late night services, conditions of carriage and it even told you where you might find your lost luggage. And all that for just 5p.

Our family's favourite pages were the ones detailing timetables for a very prestigious service indeed - The Outer Circle route. You could pack your lunch and spend the best part of a day on this bus as it cruised around parts of your home city which you never knew existed. The aim of everyone riding on this cream and blue dream machine was to get seats upstairs, as near to the front as possible.

The Outer Circle no doubt helped folk without cars to get to work and visit relatives in hospital, but during school holidays it was often full of families enjoying an afternoon out.

SHEFFIELD AREA BUS & RAIL TIMETABLE

5p

SEPTEMBER 1971 UNTIL APRIL 1972 OR FURTHER NOTICE

The route took in Barkers Pool, Hunters Bar, Crosspool, Rivelin Valley, Rustlings Road, Ecclesall, Graves Park, Meadowhead, Prince of Wales Road, Darnall, Tinsley, Wincobank, Bellhouse Road, Moonshine Lane, Penistone Road and Malin Bridge. The total journey time for route No 2 was an hour and 52 minutes.

Even before the days of deregulation, Sheffield city centre was visited by buses and coaches from a variety of other transport companies. Do you remember Booth & Fisher buses, based at Halfway, which linked Sheffield with Coal Aston, Dronfield, Apperknowle, Eckington, Killamarsh and through to Worksop? Then there were the familiar green double-deckers from Chesterfield which shared routes with Sheffield Transport.

The streets of Sheffield welcomed buses from Yorkshire Traction, West Riding Automobile Co, Hebble from Liversidge, Rotherham Corporation, Blue Line from Doncaster, Dearneway Coaches based in Goldthorpe, East Midland Motor Services, Henry Hulley based at Baslow, Wigmore's of Dinnington.

The 1971 timetable pictured included two warnings for passengers. One provided guidelines for people who found themselves on board a one-man bus for the first time, the other was a special note of an "experimental pedestrian precinct" at Fargate with all services being temporarily diverted to run via Leopold Street and Church Street. We wonder how long the experiment will go on for?

ONE-MAN BUSES

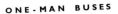

Many services are now operated by **ONE-MAN** buses:

Before boarding	1	Give a clear signal to the driver in good time.
	2	Have the exact fare (or your permit in lieu) ready in your hand.
When you board	3	Place the money on the driver's tray, not in the coin compartments, or show him your permit and take your ticket, which must be kept for inspection.
	4	Move away from the driver as soon as you have your ticket, so as not to delay people behind you. On double deck buses, if you find that the top deck is full please go downstairs at once as standing is not allowed upstairs.
When you wish to alight	5	Ring the bell *ONCE* in good time. (Do not ring it again if you have already heard someone else do so)
	6	If the bus has only one door (which will be alongside the driver) wait just behind him, so as not to obstruct his view.
	7	If the bus has two doors, you must get out of the *CENTRE* exit, so as not to delay boarding passengers.
After alighting	8	Let go of any handrails and stand clear.
	9	*NEVER* attempt to board at the centre exit, as this would be dangerous.

Your co-operation will speed the service. Please remember—wherever possible—to have the exact fare ready. Parents are also asked to supply children with the correct change for the journey to school. Change giving is the biggest cause of delay at busy times.

Europe's Strange Effect on Dave

Ask Sheffield's Dave Berry to name his favourite year and you would expect him to select 1964, the year of his massive 'Crying Game' hit - but you would be wrong. He tells Mike Firth what happened next

My Kind of Year

1965

NO-ONE in the music or entertainment business can ever be certain of the direction their careers may twist and turn and that was most certainly the case for those of us singing and playing in bands in the early 1960s.

None of us really expected things to last and it wasn't until I had survived an initial three years as a performer that I began to think that, with a little care and attention, I might make a career out of it.

The autumn of 1964 had been an excellent time for me with 'The Crying Game' taking me towards the top of the charts and by the time the following year began I was back in the recording studio looking to follow up its success with another big hit. I recorded a couple of singles and although they were not as successful, I continued to be in demand and was a regular on TV's pop programmes of the time, such as 'Ready, Steady Go' and 'Thank Your Lucky Stars'.

In early 1965 I toured the country with my band The Cruisers, together with The Rolling Stones, but there was no big forward plan for me to do anything apart from more recording sessions for Decca, more concerts and more TV performances which I really enjoyed.

There was nothing to suggest that 1965 was going to be such a landmark year for my career - and for my life in general.

When my agent Danny Betesch asked me if I would be interested in travelling with other Decca artists to Knokke in Belgium to take part in an annual international song festival in May, it was really no big deal for me. It wasn't the sort of thing I would normally have considered and if I'd had a prior booking with The Cruisers for that particular week I wouldn't have even considered it.

However, I agreed to go over with other members of the Decca team including Adrienne Posta and jazz singer Joy Marshall and I remember we flew from Southend to Knokke in a small transporter-type plane. Radio presenter Alan Freeman was also with us in the hotel in Knokke.

I had never heard of the event before - I don't think anyone on the rock and roll side of music would have done - but it was a type of mini-European Song contest with acts from Belgium, Holland, France and Germany also taking part. It was an established televised festival held in a large casino in Knokke and everyone except me wore formal evening suits and dickie-bows.

In 1960 you could book Dave Berry and his band The Cruisers to play at Doncaster Baths for £10... by 1965 Dave was famous across Europe

172, Robin Lane,
Beighton,
Nr. Sheffield.

20th. November, 1960.

Dear Sir,

This is to confirm the booking for the Cruisers and myself to appear at the Doncaster Baths Hall on Saturday, 26th. November, 3rd., 10th. and 17th. December, for an agreed sum of £10 (Ten pounds) per session.

Yours faithfully,

D Berry

To :-

Robin Eldridge,
46, Hatfield Lane
Armthorpe.
Doncaster.

Dave Berry and The Cruisers

Fan Club Newsletter

Hello again,

Once again Josie has asked me to let you know what's been happening to Dave and the Cruisers during the last month.

First of all Dave went to Belgium for a week, where he appeared in the largest hall in Brussels for one week. We had a fantastic time and on the opening day 40 policemen were called in to control the fans. It was really frightening because over there the police have guns and they look very powerful. The show ended with the police firing their guns in the air and the manager carrying Dave off the stage.

We flew from Brussels to Amsterdam where we were met by the Cruisers who had flown out from Manchester. While in Holland we did 7 shows in 3 days, and they were really tiring. At the end of the 3 days we were really tired but really happy the way the Dutch people had greeted Dave and the boys. Incidentally while Dave was in Holland he opened a new record shop in a town called Zwolle. When we arrived we could hardly believe our eyes. There were 5,000 people in the streets around the shop. Apparently the schools had been given a holiday and a car firm had been closed because of Dave's visit. Many shop windows were broken and about 20 people were injured when the crowd rioted.

There was great Press interest and I remember being flown on to Luxembourg to chat to the DJs of Radio Luxembourg.

From the outset I had decided that I would do my usual Dave Berry performance at Knokke, so I simply treated it as just another gig. I'm sure Decca thought it would be nothing more than an opportunity to promote my new single, 'This Strange Effect', which had been written for me by Ray Davies of The Kinks.

I didn't take the Micky out of the event but neither did I take it too seriously. I performed my usual strange repertoire as I would have done anywhere else, hiding behind my hands, scratching my head and slowly picking something up off the stage as I sang, and there was a real buzz in the concert hall.

Much to my surprise, the audience took to my act straight away, even though some of the international judges labelled me as being 'immoral' and a danger to teenagers because I hadn't been wearing evening dress. The Decca team didn't win anything but I was extremely proud to pick up the prestigious Press Prize, voted for by journalists from throughout Europe.

I knew the audience had loved my performance and after the show I took a walk on my own around the beautiful seaside town of Knokke until about 2am, well aware that something really important had just happened in my career.

Audiences in Holland and Belgium saw the humorous side of my stage performance and went for it one hundred per cent. They smiled when they saw me and I was delighted because I had always intended my stage show to be a little bit tongue-in-cheek.

Just a few months after my success in Knokke, I was invited to sing at the big annual music show in Holland, the Grande Gala du Disque, at the Ria Centre in Amsterdam. That was again a very special experience for me, performing on the same bill as Diana Ross and The Supremes, The Everly Brothers, The Crickets, Cilla Black and other top performers from the continent.

'This Strange Effect' was a massive hit for me in both the Dutch and Belgian charts. In Holland it remained in the top 40 for 35 weeks and I received a Gold Disc for sales of more than 100,000. At one stage I had five of my records in the charts across the

Dave became the biggest thing in the Dutch and Belgian charts in 1965

Nederlandse Hitparade december 1965

1. This Strange Effect - Dave Berry
2. Get off of my Cloud - The Rolling Stones
3. Sophietje - Johnny Lion
4. Here it comes again - The Fortunes
5. I'm gonna take you there - Dave Berry
6. Als ik de golven aan het strand zie - Ria Valk
7. You've got your Troubles - The Fortunes
8. Elke dag denk ik aan zondag - Willeke Alberti
9. Don't let the Stars... - Canadian Sweethaerts
10. Can I get it from you - Dave Berry
11. Capri c'est fini - Hervé Villard
12. Sittin' all alone - The Pretty Things
13. Een meisje van zestien - Boudewijn de Groot
14. A walk in the Black Forrest - Horst Jankowski
15. Ride Away - Roy Orbison
16. What's new Pussycat - Tom Jones
17. Little Things - Dave Berry
18. Englands Swings - Roger Miller
19. It's good news Week - Hedgehoppers Anonymous
20. Wasted Words - The Motions.

continent. And it didn't stop there. I appeared on many Dutch TV shows and even hosted my own programme where my guests included Tom Jones and The Fortunes.

The reaction towards me from young Dutch fans was truly amazing and one personal appearance I made in Amsterdam turned into something of a riot with thousands of people pursuing me through the city centre. The event was even screened on Pathe News and nowadays it makes fascinating viewing on YouTube!

Later in 1965 I was asked to perform at major venues in Copenhagen, Stockholm, Hamburg and Paris - all on the back of my success at Knokke.

Although I had taken big steps forward in all my years as a performer, 1965 saw me make a giant leap with my career. I was selling hundreds of thousands of records across the continent, 'Little Things' was a big hit for me in Britain and I had the type of bargaining power with my record company that other artists could only dream about.

To crown everything, 1965 was also the year I met my wife-to-be Marthy.

My fans on the continent have been with me for more than 45 years and I am extremely grateful to them for their support. I still perform regularly in both Holland and Belgium and whenever I cross the channel I always remember my trip to the song festival in Knokke. That event galvanised my career - and to think that at the time I was not really concerned about making the trip at all!

• Copies of Dave's illustrated autobiography, 'All There Is To Know', are available from Heron Publications on 0114 2357777 or local bookshops including Waterstone's, price £14.99.

So, what else happened in the year 1965?

• Former Prime Minister Sir Winston Churchill died on January 24th.
• A gallon - not a litre - of petrol cost five shillings (25 pence).
• Sir Stanley Matthews played his final First Division game, aged of 50 years and five days.
• Goldie, a London Zoo golden eagle, was recaptured 12 days after her escape.
• Great Train Robber Ronnie Biggs escaped from Wandsworth Prison and fled to Brazil.
• Cosmonaut Aleksei Leonov became the first person to walk in space.
• The Mary Quant-designed mini skirt first appeared in London.
• Liverpool won the FA Cup, beating Leeds United 2-1 in the final.
• Muhammad Ali knocked out Sonny Liston in the first round of their rematch.
• Edward Heath became leader of the Conservative Party.
• Thunderbirds and Tom & Jerry both made their debuts on TV.
• The Post Office Tower opened in London.

Sheffield's favourite comedian Bobby Knutt reflects on various parts of his life in this regular My Kind of Town feature

Sunday splodgin'

All aboard the ferry at Stixwould

WHEN my pal John Firminger asked me for a small contribution to the new 'My Kind of Town' mag, I was both chuffed and honoured. The first page of my book 'Eyup Knutty' expresses my love for Sheffield and I quote: "To be born a Sheffielder is to have won first prize in the lottery of life."

Here is an excerpt from an early chapter which relates my trips with my father fishing on the River Witham in Lincolnshire with thousands of other Sheffield "maggot drownders".

My dad was one, and I started going fishing with him when I was about five years old. We'd go on Sunday and walk down to Victoria Station which was a good two miles from our house. My dad would carry the fishing basket over his shoulder. It contained all the tackle, the tin of maggots, the sandwiches and the flask of tea. I'd carry the rods in their canvas bags and I'd keep changing shoulders as they were bloody heavy for a little lad to carry.

We'd leave about 4.15am and it was always dark. I always remember my Dad would creep silently up to the attic where I was in deep slumber and gently shake me awake. I'd come downstairs and he'd have a cup of tea and a dripping sandwich waiting for me.

The journey to the station took us past Davy's bakery (bottom of Charles Street) and the smell of the fresh-baked loaves coming out of the big ovens was my favourite smell of all.

The trains laid on for the anglers were the 'fishermen's specials' and I think there was about three of them that left at 15 minute intervals, starting at 4.45am. They headed into Lincolnshire to the little stations dotted along the banks of the River Witham. My dad always chose a little place called Stixwould; he reckoned it was the best place for the bream he loved to catch.

I used to love going 'splodgin', as fishing was affectionately called by all Sheffielders. My dad would tramp along the embankment that ran along the river so as to choose his fishing hole, or 'oil', as it was known.

"Are we there yet Dad?" I'd winge. "No, t'best oils are a bit further up", he'd quietly reply.

Once he'd decided on a good spot, we'd have to bash a pathway through the thick barrier of stinging nettles that lined the bankside. I didn't get my first pair of long trousers until I was 12 so you can imagine the state of my little legs by the time we got to the river. I'd be nettled to bloody death and trying not to cry in front of my dad. He'd tell me to go and find some dock leaves and rub the stings with then.

Once we got tackled up and cast out it was time for me to "Shurrup". You can't talk when you're fishing 'cause it "freetens t'fish". I was a right chatterbox when I was a kid and I was incurably curious about everything and anything. My Dad was the

most patient and understanding person I ever knew, but he'd eventually say "Go and pester Mr Martin".

Stixwould was one of the only places on the river that had a ferry which meant you could get to the other side if you so wished. It was for foot passengers, and it was overseen by Mr Martin who also worked the signal box at the adjacent station. Mrs Martin used to make pots of tea for thirsty fishermen; it was so strong, you could trot a mouse across it.

The ferry was wound from one side of the river to the other by a big metal handle which, when turned furiously, would crank the rickety contraption across the water. I very soon talked Mr Martin into allowing me to crank the handle as he took a rest and after a few weeks, I was promoted to regular ferryman.

> 'Mrs Martin used to make pots of tea for thirsty fishermen. It was so strong you could trot a mouse across it'

There was a bell on each side of the river to attract the attention of the ferryman, so on hearing the ringing, I'd be there, winding that great handle for dear life to get there as fast as I could. Mrs Martin would provide the sustenance for my efforts; she'd make me big doorstep corned beef sandwiches which I washed down with a bottle of Tizer.

There were no corridors on those old fishing trains so once we set off, that was it, no toilets, no buffet car. There'd be eight men with all their fishing tackle crammed into the single compartment and I'd be in my element listening to all the adult conversations and all the farts which seemed to come with alarming regularity causing much laughter amongst us all.

It's funny how in those days nobody ever bothered about suncream. We'd no idea about skin cancer so we just didn't use a sun block. My old man was very fair-skinned and he was bald. I never ever remember him having any hair; he had a bit round the sides and back, but none on top. By the end of the day his poor nut would be bright red and so would my exposed bits. When we got back home my mam would rub calamine lotion on us both to soothe the burning.

The Sunday fishing trip was a great adventure for me and it's one of my fondest memories as a lad.

• Eyup Knutty; The Life & Loves of a Stand Up Comic, ALD Design & Print, ISBN 978-1-901587-79-1, £9.99.

EYUP KNUTTY
The Life & Loves of a Stand Up Comic
The Years 1945-1981
Bobby Knutt

When 'The Twang' returned to town

Grammy Award-winning guitarist Duane Eddy has made a couple of visits to Sheffield. The first was way back in 1960 when he performed at the old Gaumont Cinema, the second was to record his brand new album in Neepsend. Honest! John Firminger tells the unlikely story

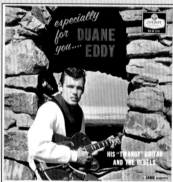

WITH his moody, almost teen-idol looks as he clutched his familiar red Gretch guitar whilst sitting in a stone alcove - this is the everlasting image I have of instrumental great Duane Eddy as seen on the cover of his second album, Especially For You.

This was, in fact, the first long-playing album I ever owned and would join the rest of the Duane Eddy records that I bought with loyal regularity as they came out.

Needless to say, I was there in my seat upstairs at the Gaumont Cinema, when Duane appeared in Sheffield in person April 7th, 1960. The date was part of a nationwide tour in the company of fellow Americans Bobby Darin and Clyde McPhatter who had the partially limited backing of Bob Miller & His Millermen whilst Duane had the advantage of having his own band, The Rebels.

It was, therefore, quite significant that 50 years on, Duane would come back to Sheffield and this time his return was just as poignant, maybe even more so. Well, for Richard Hawley it certainly was as the local musical hero and the legendary guitarist would be combining their talents to record an album together.

Richard is a huge fan of Duane and also the guitarist's former producer and co-writer, Lee Hazlewood. In fact, whilst Richard is recognised as one of the foremost talents in today's music world, he has a deep love and admiration for many of the classic and vintage performers, inherited from his guitarist dad, the late Dave Hawley.

However, it was Richard's manager Graham Wrench, also a Duane fan, who was the key figure behind Duane and Richard's amalgam. After long-distance phone conversations, Graham ended up becoming Duane's European representative and proved his worth by setting up a short but high profile tour of the UK.

Using Richard's accomplished band to back Duane on the tour, part of the arrangement would naturally also be to get Duane in the studio. As the live performances had certainly attracted the media and fans alike towards Duane's music again, so a proposed new album, combining Richard and Duane's talent would also see the man enjoying a new lease of life.

Actually that would be an incorrect term, as Duane's music has always sound fresh and vibrant and has been constant though the years. Emerging in various musical settings, recording and performing with people like The Art Of Noise, George Harrison, Paul McCartney, Ry Cooder and The Mavericks through to successful film soundtracks like Pulp Fiction, subconsciously,

Duane's music has always been there.

Going back to those great instrumentals, Shazam!, Forty Miles Of Bad Road, Some Kinda Earthquake, Kommotion, etc, as soon as they were released I bought em' all. Playing them, I'd look longingly at every detail printed out on the record label.

Recorded in Phoenix, Arizona, Hollywood and Nashville, these places conjured up great images of hip and exotic recording studios in spacious locations and the cool musicians who helped Duane to make the tracks so special. Therefore the concept of Duane actually recording in my home town would be like some wonderful surreal dream.

Fast forward something like 45 years and such a dream became reality when Richard impressed Duane enough to actually make the trip to Sheffield to record and reiterate the title of Duane's first album, 'Have Twangy Guitar Will Travel'.

The journey would see Duane bringing that twangy guitar from one of the acknowledged music capitals of the world, Nashville, all the way to the industrial area of Neepsend at the Yellow Arch Studio. Whether the old brick building and cobbled yard is a far cry from the kind of modern lay-out of Nashville is totally irrelevant as it's what comes out of the studio that matters of course.

This is Richard's usual recording location and has proved its worth with the success of his own acclaimed albums 'Coles Corner', 'Low Edges', 'Lady's Bridge' and 'Truelove's Gutter'.

In the studio, through his musical tenacity, he's also brought renewed attention to Tony Christie and Nancy Sinatra. In fact there's another connection there as Nancy's hit period of the 1960s was masterminded by Lee Hazlewood.

Duane is of course familiar with Richard's work and impressed by the quality of the recordings. He commented: "It's a big sound and I just wanted to get in on some of it."

Impressed enough with the Sheffield set-up also, he went as far as saying on TV: "We might even look for some property here".

Working together in the studio, and with a fairly tight time schedule, everybody displayed great creativity. Richard managed to come up with no fewer than 18 numbers for consideration whilst the band also chipped in with a few ideas of their own.

For their work on stage and in the studio, credit should certainly be given to Colin Elliott, bass-player and Richard's co-producer, guitarist Shez Sheridan, drummer Dean Beresford and pianist John Trier. Also making a most valid contribution is Ron Dziubla, the young world-class American saxophonist who Duane brought over

Did you know... in 1960, readers of New Musical Express voted Duane Eddy the 'World's No 1 Musical Personality', ousting Elvis Presley?

Partners... Sheffield's Richard Hawley welcomes Duane Eddy to his home town

with him. He certainly confirmed the sax's key role in Duane's music. Ron's own album Some Strange Blues certainly puts his instrument through its paces, so much so some cuts warrant a government health-warning, re-defining the terms, wail, growl and honk!

Once the sessions with Duane were completed, Richard regained some slack by calling into his favourite hostelry, Fagan's, a most conducive pub for creative people and discerning drinkers. Duane and his wife, Deed, obligingly joined Richard to sample some of the warm hospitality and unassuming ambience as created by hosts Tom and Barbara Boulding. It's quite a heart-warming thought to know that such a legendary figure as Duane has actually been in one of the pubs I go in!

Meeting local fans like Pete Jackson, Duane was highly amused and amazed when Pete reeled off all the musicians who've been associated with Duane both onstage and on record back in the 'golden days'. In fact, the next time that Duane might require somebody to provide the familiar 'Rebel yells' either on stage or record, Pete's yer man!

Another of Duane's links with Sheffield is one Arthur Moir, a college professor and lecturer, who, away from his academic duties, runs the Duane Eddy Circle UK from his home in Lodge Moor. Keeping a watchful eye on all Duane's activities, Arthur keeps everyone informed via the Circle's publication 'Twangsville'. Duane's last UK visit certainly kept the Circle on its toes with so much media coverage with Arthur managing to serve his main man well, keeping on top of it all with the magazine and global emails.

The October 2010 Yellow Arch sessions will emerge in album form under the title of Road Trip, released on June 20th, 2011, on Mad Monkey Records - in conjunction with EMI and co-produced by Richard Hawley. Containing 11 songs recorded in 11 days, it's a fine effort from all involved, commencing with the primal rocker 'The Attack Of The Duck Billed Platypus' and firmly in the Duane Eddy mode. The neatly titled 'Twango' is a tribute to the great 'gypsy of jazz' Django Reinhardt.

There's plenty more of the great man's trademark 'Twang' on 'Curveball', and a slice of garage rock 'n' roll with 'Primeval' filled with deep twang and wailing sax, again in true Eddy tradition. 'Kindness Ain't Made Of Sand' is a fine representation of Duane and Richard's styles coming together on a piece they co-wrote.

Adding a further touch of South Yorkshire is 'Mexborough Ferry Boat Halt', a piece written by Mexborough-born Shez Sheridan as a tribute to his dad. Redressing the balance is a title relating to Duane's Tennessee home town, the beautifully picked and understated album-closer, 'Franklin Town'.

Throughout it all, the album continues to remind us of the mighty guitar-playing and writing talents of Duane Eddy. It also marks the legendary guitarist's first studio album for 24 years whilst also adding a touch of classic rock 'n' roll credibility to Sheffield's own musical tapestry.

Who's that knocking at the door?

Margaret Shaw grew up in Sheffield in the 1940s when it was customary for local traders and salesmen to visit people 'door-to-door' to secure their business. Here she recalls some of the characters who were regular visitors to her home

IF anyone knocks at our door these days many of us hesitate and are wary about who it might be before we open the door to greet them. But it was not so in the 'olden days'.

The first person to call at our Sheffield home in the morning would be the postman/woman, then around lunchtime they would return with a second delivery. One of my aunts was a postwoman before she joined the ATS during World War II. Seeing her in her uniform, I thought "that's what I want to do when I grow up."

The milkman would call mid-morning, arriving in a small van and carrying the milk to the door in a small churn. He would have three measures; a third-of-a-pint, half-pint and pint. He would pour milk into the measure and my mother would have a jug waiting for him to pour it into. His name was Mr Morton and I believe he came from Grindleford. Can anyone else remember him?

The rent lady, Miss Barton, called once a fortnight for her money and when the gas and electric men visited us they had to go down into the cellar to read the meters. Our supply was "penny in the slot" and when the supply was running low we had to go into the cellar and put pennies into a meter, turning a knob after each one dropped.

The man would empty all the pennies into a bag, carry them up the cellar steps, empty them out onto the table and count them into piles. Then he would put them into £1 paper bags and place them into his big leather bag.

The paper boys would be round twice each day, delivering The Sheffield Telegraph in the morning and The Star at night.

A window cleaner visited us once a fortnight and I remember his services cost 1/4d.

The dustbinmen arrived once a week, carrying a large oval metal container on their shoulders, with a handle on each end. They emptied each bin into it and carried it out to the lorry in the road.

Do you remember when every house had regular visits from the coalman? My grandparents and parents had their coal delivered by Benny Darvill and his son, Len. After I married, we had coal delivered by Mr Wilkinson.

The coal would arrive by rail at the large goods yard at Meersbrook where the retail centre now stands. Each coal merchant had his own little office and the coal was weighed into sacks with 1cwt in each. Then it was loaded onto lorries and taken out for delivery. Our coal was dropped down the cellar-grate at the front of our terraced house.

With most people in Sheffield having coal fires, the chimney-sweep was in great demand. The one we used would tell the children to go outside into the street and watch for his brush popping out of the chimney-pots.

Another regular visitor to our house was the insurance man, calling for his "tuppence per person per week".

Can anyone else recall on Saturday afternoons a man visiting their home carrying a large basket covered with a white cloth? He sold oatcakes and pikelets.

Ice-cream man Taggy was a most welcome visitor to any Sheffield street. More about him in the next edition of 'My Kind of Town'

Taggy was by far the most popular visitor of the week, serving his delicious Sheffield-made ice-cream from his large decorated van. He made ice-cream before World War II and resumed once the war was over.

The ragman was another visitor to our street with his wooden barrow. I don't know how he pushed it up and down the steep roads in some parts of Sheffield but I remember his call "Donkey-stone for rags". Donkey-stone and yellow-stone was used to clean the window-sills and doorsteps and most women took a pride in that job. I was allowed to put the white edge on using "white cardinal" - "red cardinal" was used for floors.

Children would dash to their mothers for old clothes because they knew the ragman would exchange them for balloons or, if they were lucky, perhaps a goldfish.

The knife-sharpener called to sharpen knives, scissors and garden-shears for a small charge.

Gipsies visited on a regular basis, selling their hand-made wooden pegs and coloured flowers made from shaved wood.

There was a nice little man who visited our home with a little brown leather case selling cottons, needles, pins and lace.

I also remember the Rington's Tea van calling to deliver tea and biscuits.

If children were absent from school their parents could expect a visit from the School Bobby, but luckily he was one man who never knocked on the door at our house.

Part One of John Firminger's personal guide to Sheffield's bands and groups of the 1950s and 1960s. How many of these do you recall seeing on stage locally?

Call up

IN this series, we go back to a golden age when the city's music scene was certainly a vibrant one. It was a time when Sheffielders enjoyed the sounds of many hundreds of combos and ensembles, whether it be served up in youth clubs, pubs, WMCs, nightclubs or any other place where live music could be played. I'm sure some of the bands and venues mentioned here will bring back plenty of happy memories.

Acid
Teenage psychedelic group who included Saturday morning butcher's boy, guitarist and future songwriter and Acoustic Angel, Carey Baylis.

Andy Capps
Schoolboy skiffle band from the Ecclesfield/Parson Cross area including future Lizard and Hillbilly Cat, Pete Jackson. One of the bands who took part in the Skiffle Contest at the Empire Theatre, Don't You Rock Me Daddy-o.

Steve Allen & The Vikings
Consisted of guitarists Keith Renwick and Grenville Hydes, singer Steve Allen, guitarist Colin Smith and drummer Ken Fielding. Despite the band's name, thankfully,they managed to restrain themselves from raping and pillaging, Up Helly Aa!

Vance Arnold & The Avengers

Vance Arnold was the name singer John Cocker had contrived for himself when he moved from playing drums to taking over singing. The band's first gig was at the Minerva Hotel in the city centre. Other members of band were bass-player Bob Everson, Steve McEnna on drums, Graham Hobson on rhythm guitar and Phil Crookes on lead. The band became regular favourites at The Greengate Inn, High Green and Fleur De Lys, Totley. With Dave Memmott on drums and Graham Bower on rhythm guitar, the band became more popular as Vance Arnold emerged as a most impressive r&b singer.

Art Gallery
Formerly known as The Male Set. Had a change of image and line-up with Stewart Middleton on lead guitar, singer Graham Boone, Adrian Middleton on bass, Bob Burnham on organ and drummer Alan Murfin. Breaking new ground the band experimented with a lighting system so that a different light reacted to each instrument. Psychedelic, man!

Atlantics
Young teen-beat trio with John Maltby on lead, bass-player Steve Skelton and rhythm guitarist Alan Burgess, plus ten-year-old drummer Kevin Loosemore who was believed to be the youngest drummer in Europe. However, this had one drawback as officially he was too young to be paid - that's show-biz kid! When Burgess and Allen decided to leave they were replaced by Kevin Mooney and Steve Allen.

Autocrats

Sheffield four-piece comprising drummer Mike Duke, lead guitarist Robert Duke, bass guitarist Brian Jackson and rhythm guitarist and singer Nev Hanson. 'Top Stars' reported them getting a gig at Blackpool Tower, although we're not sure if it was *in* it or *up* it!

The Barons
Originally formed by bass-player Barry Cosgrove when he was in the RAF in Aden. He reformed the band with Sheffield musicians, Phil Saunders on lead, organist Keith Gale, rhythm guitarist Tony Ford and Frank Fisher on drums.

Dave Berry & The Cruisers

Originally formed in 1960 by ex-members of Frantic Four and quickly became extremely popular locally before Dave and the band scored their first hit with their recording of 'Memphis Tennessee'. Dave, of course, went onto become Sheffield's first international star and continues to enjoy a successful career in music. Other hits included 'Baby It's You', 'My Baby Left Me', 'This Strange Effect', 'Little Things' and, of course, 'The Crying Game'. Always credited as a top backing band, during the 1960s The Cruisers included such acclaimed Sheffield musicians as guitarists Frank Miles (ex-Frantic Four), Alan Taylor, John Fleet, Roy Barber (ex-Mariners), Kenny Slade, Frank White (ex-Ravens), Roy Ledger (ex-Sheffields), John Riley (ex-Debonaires), Pete Cliffe (ex-Vampires), Roger Jackson (ex-Lizards). In 1965 The Cruisers also had a record out in their own right featuring 'It Ain't Me Babe'/'Baby, What Do You Want Me To Do?'.

The Big Four

Although they were together for only one gig, the Sun Sound Club Rock 'n' Country Jamboree at the City Hall Ballroom in April '67, the band sported quite a significant line-up of four of Sheffield's most respected musicians. On rhythm guitar was future agent Alan Wood, ex-Stroller Mal Hooley on bass and John Riley on drums and vocals, with Frank White on vocals and lead guitar and looking really dashing on the night in a bright red guardsman's tunic.

the groups

Bitter Suite

Briefly previously known as Jigsaw before another group of that name ordered them to change. A band of various guises from pop to a seven-piece soul band to hard rockin' four-piece combo. Throughout their many musical changes they were extremely popular with club audiences and were also featured many times performing live on Radio 2. They had several record releases but for varying reasons

could never seem to achieve any success and simply relied on the endless round of clubs and cabaret for work. Long-standing singer Barry Marshall was formerly with Dean Marshall & Deputies and Lizards. Barry fronted the band through its different phases from an eight-piece soul band to a hard driving four-piece rock unit. Joining Barry throughout the various changes was bass-player Gerry Scanlon (also from Lizards). Other members of Bitter Suite through the years included sax players Mick Bell and Vic Middleton, trumpeter Ian Brooks, organist Adrian Askew, drummers Mick Wilkinson, Tommy Sloan, Neil Wathey and Steve 'Bubbles' Mitchell, guitarists Ray Ashton, John Parr and Phil Brodie, keyboardist Ivor Drawmer and Stuart Singleton. The band had several records released but unfortunately never achieved any great success.

Black Cats

Three-man skiffle group who included guitarist/singer from Darnall, Dave Hawley.

Bloos Express

Teenage soul-type outfit with vocalist Martin Brennan, Ian Wyles on lead guitar, David Tyler, Stephen Padley and Roger Loxley. Following the soul music trend, this five-piece group had ambitions of developing

into a big band with no limit in size. Yeah, but that breaks the money down a bit. Undaunted by this prospect they eventually brought in sax player Alan Penn and trumpeter Kenneth Gordon.

Blues By Seven

R&B septet made up of musicians from Sheffield University Jazz Band and Eddie Speight Combo with Vic Lundy on on trumpet and harmonica, Dave Green on stick-bass, Mack White on vocals, Dixie Dean on tenor sax, Eddie Speight on guitar, Dick Marsden on drums and Alex White on piano.

Blueberries

Chesterfield rhythm & blues band whose drummer was also music writer and DJ David McPhie and who played a major role in helping to get Joe Cocker on record in 1967. The band later moved into soul

music with Jeff Fountain on rhythm and bass, Jim MaGuire on bass and sax and singer Ian Lee incorporating a dance routine. As a soul band they had a record issued by Mercury 'It's Gonna Work Out Fine'/'Please Don't Let Me Know'. When singer Ian Lee became Ian LeRoy the band became Ian LeRoy's Spring Collection in view of the female attention he was getting. Well he was a quite good looking, clean and smart young man.

Blue Diamonds

Skiffle group of 14 year-olds including guitarists Neil Bridges and Andy Mignon. The group were one of the many entrants in Nation Skiffle Contest at Empire Theatre and also made appearances at Regal Cinema, Attercliffe. Through winning a local skiffle contest in 1957 they must have been one of the first local groups to make a record when they made an acetate recording in a small studio above Curtis's Record Shop on London Road of "It Takes A Worried Man" which seemingly contained about 30 verses.

Border River Scuffle Combo

Frecheville skiffle group including John Greaves who later took on the name of Johnny Tempest.

Breakdown Blues Band

Group of Sheffield University students with Ray Woolfendon on lead guitar, Paul Jeavons on drums, Alan McCaffrey on bass, Keith Wiser on vocals and guitar and Stef on organ. The Hermitage Inn at the bottom of London Road was their regular stomping ground.

Tom Brown's Schooldays

Bluesy-progressive five-piece with singer Jay Jones, drummer Terry Jones, guitarist Ronnie Hay, bass-player Dave Morton and lead guitarist Steve Mellor. Boasted a fan-club of 50 strong, which is handy for helping to carry the gear in.

The Cadillacs

Original band formed by John Wilson on bass along with Barry Brumpton on lead guitar, Tom Rattigan on rhythm, John Hall on drums and singer Bob. A change of line-up saw singer Johnny Tempest and Chris Stainton on bass join from the Mariners and Malc Towndrow replacing Rattigan. With this line-up the band became very popular around the local pub scene with Tempests' version of High Noon being a particular highlight which usually made the girls all swoon. Ah!

Can Of Beans

Featuring guitarist George Gill in this R&B combo with a tinny sound.

The Cargills

Country/rock duo featuring two excellent guitarists and singers Dave Hawley and Ron Blythe. Dave had previously been with international cabaret and recording act, The Lorne Gibson Trio and Ron with Glen Dale's Candies. Inevitably,

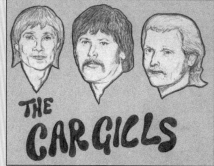

they were later joined by one John Firminger on drums and relished the days when they all had plenty of hair.

The Cavaliers

Young Sheffield rock group whose drummer was John Cocker, later known as Vance Arnold and Joe Cocker. Other members of group were Phil Crookes (guitar), Bob Everson (bass) and John Mitchell (guitar).

The Chains

Sheffield group featuring flame-haired girl singer Janet Davenport, lead guitarist Roger Fowler, bass-player Dave Fitzpatrick and drummer Neil Shaw. The band played in front of 37,000 people when they performed on the pitch at Bramall Lane prior to the

United v Wednesday derby. Unfortunately the band's set was cut short due to Roger burning his fingers when a short occurred in their equipment which in view of the venue was classed as a shock result.

The Chains

Sharing the same name, this version was from down the river and the Rotherham-based combo was one of a number of bands that charismatic singer Pete Fender worked with.

Checkers

Showy Sheffield skiffle group who were seven-strong at one point in their brief career and played at Farm Grounds Talent Contest and the National Skiffle Contest at The Empire. They were also a regular attraction at the infamous, yet much remembered, El Mambo coffee-bar on Union Street. Line-up included singer Tony Copley, guitarist Stuart McKenzie, lead guitar, Greg Eames, Geoff 'Slats' Slater, bass-guitar, Alan Smith, bass and washboard-player/singer Jim Greaves later of cabaret/ club act The Barton Brothers.

Chequers

Adding a bit of variety, this Rawmarsh-based band featured Elvis-like singer Wilf Broadhead and girl vocalist Maureen Byrnes along with Martin Willingham on bass, Roy Eades on rhythm, Colin Smith on drums and Steve Ibbotson on lead. Moving into clubland, the band made the life-changing decision to change their name to The Chequers Show and with this came a new set of stage-clothes. These kind of things happen in showbiz.

Chicago Line

Another of the local soul bands to emerge and who came under the managerial wing of Peter Stringfellow. The band recorded their version of Little Anthony's "Shimmy, Shimmy Ko-Ko-Bop".

Bass guitarist Graham Lampshire was joined by vocalist Phil Kay, lead guitarist Terry Hooson and drummer Stuart O'Connor.

The Cherokees

Fronted originally by singer Dave West, the band was runner-up in the 1963 Mackeson Beat Contest. Later continuing as a four-piece, members included Roger Harrison (drums) and

songwriter Pete Jowell (guitar), with bassist Tony Martin and ex-Avenger Graham Bower. The band was subsequently joined by powerhouse girl singer Jean 'Georgia' Rodgers who recorded one of Pete Jowell's songs 'Baby What You Gonna Do?' for Columbia Records.

The Chevrons

With ex-Strollers guitarist Roy Ledger, drummer John Lofthouse, rhythm-guitarist Dave 'Rusty' Rogers and bass player Chris Ives and singer Dave Bradley. Band held down a successful summer season in Blackpool in '63, arranged for them by Dave Berry.

After band split, Ledger went with Sheffields, Lofthouse joined Greycats, Ives became Dave Berry's roadie and Rogers later be Frank White's manager.

Chicago Line

Another of the local soul bands to emerge and who came under the managerial wing of Peter Stringfellow. The band recorded their version of Little Anthony's 'Shimmy, Shimmy Ko-Ko-Bop'. Bass guitarist Graham Lampshire was joined by vocalist Phil Kay, lead guitarist Terry Hooson and drummer Stuart O'Connor.

Citadels

Named after St Aiden's Church Hall, where the name Citadel was enscribed above the door. Named as such by Peter Stringfellow who managed the band and of course had his first venue The Black Cat Club there. The band would get dressed up in horror garb and go out as The Skeletons, backing band of Count Lindsay III. Included in line-up were guitarists Keith 'Mo' Linacre and Ray Ashton. Another line-up consisted of Bob Grundy on guitar and Dave 'Cannon' Smith on drums together with singer Pete Fender and Mal Hooley on bass from the Farinas.

The Citizens

Rotherham based mod-soul combo with singer Graham Boone, drummer Dave Bennett, bass-player Ray Hodgson, Stewart Middleton on lead and his brother Adrian on rhythm. With their brightly painted group van they claimed to have the first pop-art vehicle in the country, being the handywork of Stewart. Way-out, man!

Dave Clifford &
The Orpheans

Unfortunately we spilt a cup-o-soup over the band's write-up in our copy of 'Top Stars' but here's a cool pic of the boys in rockin' pose to compensate.

Climax Jazzmen

Stomping six-piece, popular in and around Sheffield with founder and leader Roger Cobbold who originally played trumpet before switching to trombone, banjo-player Bobby Slater, Harry Jervis on bass, drummer Tony Pigott, Terry Hodgson on trumpet and aptly-named clarinet player Acker Senior.

Ron Lindsay & The Coasters

Featuring singer Ronald James Williams Crawford Lindsay who was joined by pianist Terry Thornton, guitarist sax-player Alan Smith and guitarist Hayden Percival, the band first got together in the canteen at Davy United's. Progressing, the line-up later featured Lindsay, Smith, Percival, together with drummer Mick Beaumont and guitarist Frank White. The band became a big favourites at the Saturday

morning Teenage Shows at the Sheffield Gaumont before blazing a trail around the dance halls. Following a successful appearance at the 2 I's coffee bar in London, the band was signed to Columbia Records and changed their name to Jimmy Crawford & The Ravens so as to not be confused with American vocal group The Coasters

Cobwebs

Formerly known as The Road Runners with guitarist Alan Townsend, bass-player Dave Robinson, guitarist Keith Helliwell, drummer Kenny Fielding and singer Ray Daveron. Subsequent line-up changes brought in Mike Brady on rhythm guitar, Ian James on piano, Mike Shepherd on lead and Jay Kent on bass.

Joe Cocker's Big Blues

After changing his name from Vance Arnold, Joe Cocker also formed a new R&B/Soul band with Dave Hopper on guitar, Dave Green on bass, Dave Memmott on drums and Vernon Nash on electric piano. With the band he also saw the release of his first record on Decca 'Ill Cry Instead'/'Precious Words'. Almost resident at the Esquire Club, whose owner Terry Thornton managed the band for three years and organised a tour of France for them playing US Air Bases. However, as the US Airmen had requested a female vocalist in the band, Sheffield girl singer Billie Rae (Marie Woodhouse) was sent over to add some glamour for the remainder of the tour which was riddled with various problems. They might have been better just dressing one of the band up in a frock with a bit of make-up?

60s Party in the Park

The sounds of the 60s come to Dronfield in a big way in the summer of 2011 with three of the decade's biggest bands playing at an outdoor concert

JULY 9th 2011 sees an event for all lovers of good time music with the Party in the Park. Staged in Cliffe Park, Callywhite Lane, Dronfield, the open-air event will see three of the greatest names of 60s music performing onstage; with Sheffield's own Dave Berry and his band The Cruisers joined by The Tremeloes and The Searchers. It's all for a great cause too with proceeds going to Bluebell Wood Children's Hospice.

It's the brain-child of local driving instructor and St John Ambulance member Derri Jones who got the idea after attending similar events out at Clumber Park.

"I just wanted to have one bash at organising something like this and raising money for a good cause at the same time," he says.

Although there will be food and drink on sale, music fans are welcome to take along their own picnics, tables and chairs.

Party in the Park organiser Derri Jones (left) with Dave Berry and Bluebell Wood's Andrea Hudson

It's quite fitting to have Dave Berry taking part in this event, being one of Sheffield's great music icons (this month he's an icon, whereas next month he informs us he'll be a legend!).

As many Sheffield music fans will recall, Dave first became popular all around the region playing at places like the Club 60, The Esquire, Victoria Ballroom in Chesterfield and Doncaster Baths. With his choice reportoire, he emerged in the 60s as one of Britain's pioneering R&B exponents as his popularity took him further afield.

This led him to a lengthy recording contract with Decca Records and he had his first hit in September 1963 with his cover of Chuck Berry's 'Memphis Tennessee'. Other hits followed by way of some quality recordings with 'My Baby Left Me', 'Baby It's You', 'Little Things', 'Mama' and of course the classic 'The Crying Game.' Another of Dave's recording was the Ray Davies' song 'This Strange Effect' and whilst it didn't register in the UK, it became the biggest selling record in Holland, making him Sheffield's first international star.

After the success of the 60s Dave, of course, became a great survivor and continued to tour and cut the occasional record, enabling him to maintain a very active and constant career. Reflecting this, Dave has just finished a prestigious nationwide 55-night tour in the company of Chris Farlowe, The Merseybeats, Wayne Fontana, Vanity Fair and Terry Sylvester.

Sporting one of pop music's most memorable stage-acts, Dave is backed up as usual by The Cruisers now featuring probably their longest serving line-up. Dave and the band continue to work all over the country and the continent whilst still enjoying a strong local following. Always well supported whenever and wherever he appears in the region, Dave is really looking forward to this event. However, as he lives in Dronfield and is an avid walker, you may see him peeking from behind a lamp-post as he walks to the gig!

Check out Dave's website: www.cryinggame.co.uk

With more than a dozen hit records to their name, The Searchers remain true legends of 60s music. They too are very active, constantly touring and enjoying immense popularity all over the world. Featuring founder member John McNally on lead guitar and vocals along with 1960s recruit Frank Allen on bass and vocals, they're joined by singer/guitarist Spencer James, who is now in his 25th year with The Searchers, and their newest member, drummer Scott Ottaway, with the band now for 18 months.

There'll be a lot of Sheffield fans who'll remember seeing The Searchers for the first time when Pete and Geoff Stringfellow brought them to St Aiden's Church Hall in 1963. At the time they were on the verge of stardom with their first record for Pye Records, 'Sweets For My Sweet' and soon would be one of the major forces in the Merseybeat phenomenon.

With original members Tony Jackson, Mike Pender, Chris Curtis and John McNally they went onto more successes with 'Sugar And Spice', 'Ain't Gonna Kiss Ya',' Needles & Pins' and 'Don't Throw Your Love Away'.

As a replacement for Tony Jackson in 1964, Frank Allen added to the band's continuing success as they developed their own highly identifiable sound. This was demonstrated on further hits like 'Someday We're Gonna Love Again', 'When You Walk In The Room', 'What Have They Done To The Rain', 'Goodbye My Love', 'He's Got No Love' and 'Take Me For What I'm Worth'.

Similar to The Beatles, they also had four EP releases which also afforded them chart status. Despite the guys themselves being a little older these days, their youthful performance should certainly lull us all into a sense of false security and make us feel like teenagers again. Check out the Searchers official website: www.the-searchers.co.uk

Originally from Dagenham, The Tremeloes also hold a great record of their own for hit singles. Beginning of course with singer Brian Poole, their early hits were influenced by the northern beat music scene with 'Twist And Shout', 'Do You Love Me?', 'Candy Man', 'Someone, Someone', 'The Three Bells' and 'I Want Candy'.

After Brian split from the band, original members, Dave Munden (drums/vocals), Alan Blakely (guitar/vocals) and Rick Westwood (guitar/vocals) were joined by singer/bass-player Len 'Chip' Hawkes. With this line-up, they reinvented themselves as a band in their own right and enjoyed even more success.

Signed up with CBS Records they had a string of chart hits which began with Cat Stevens' effervescent 'Here Comes My Baby'. Other chart placings saw some more great pop hits of the mid to late 60s with 'Silence Is Golden', 'Even The Bad Times Are Good', 'Suddenly You Love Me', 'My Little Lady', 'I Shall Be Released', 'Hello World' and '(Call Me) Number One'.

The Trems' line-up today consists of original members Dave and Rick along with Joe Gillingham (keyboards/vocals) a member since 1988 and Jeff Brown (bass/vocals) who joined in 2004. As you'll see and hear, they do great justice to those magnificent hits whilst still boasting plenty of hair, and fairly trim waist-lines, with their tight leather trousers also helping them to hit those high notes.

Check out The Trems' own website at: www.thetremeloes.co.uk

Also re-charging his batteries and coming out of retirement for the event is Alan Gee, one-time Sheffield DJ from such haunts as The Fiesta and Tiffany's. He'll be keeping everything 'fab'n'groovy' and playing some of his favourite 60s tracks, although having now switched to CD as opposed to his trusty old disco-decks.

With Dronfield playing host to such a major star-studded event and with all the great music in prospect, it should be a great turn-out as the area truly becomes 'pop-tastic'. It certainly deserves to be, especially as the event is supporting such a very worthwhile cause.

Sponsored by one of our sister magazines, Dronfield Eye, the July 9th Party in the Park will run from 4-11pm with tickets being sold through Bluebell Wood, tel 01909 517360, www.bluebellwood.org

Bespoke Blinds & Poles Ltd

Your home, your windows, your style---*our help...*

Inspiring Windows
all over South Yorkshire

Bespoke Blinds & Poles has two showrooms, at Beauchief and Hillsborough.

They have established themselves as one of the leading suppliers of window and conservatory blinds, curtain poles and tracks and plantation shutters, with one of the most comprehensive displays of these products in South Yorkshire and NE Derbyshire.

Bespoke Blinds are the only Inspiration Dealers for Luxaflex Blinds in South Yorkshire, "The status itself may not mean anything to our customers", writes owner Maxine Hayter, "but it reflects in our showrooms and the quality and variety of products that our customers can choose from". They pride themselves on their knowledge of domestic blinds and plantation shutters, and showcase the full range of products for this brand.

Luxaflex® Inspiration

S:CRAFT

"Our customers are often looking for something a little different, an investment in the home rather than a "quick fix". Many Luxaflex products offer a unique way of dressing a window, whilst being practical, useable and safe." They are also authorised dealers of S:Craft shutters.

"To help you meet your project timetables, it's a really good idea to bring approx. measurements for your windows when you visit the showroom. It helps you identify the most suitable products for your windows, and allows you to get a ball-park cost for budgetary considerations."suggests Maxine.

Customers from as far away as London trust Maxine and Neil to get the job done as they have such an excellent reputation for providing a service that is second-to-none. Maxine said: "We pride ourselves on being the kind of company which can do what everyone else says is impossible.

"It's a really exciting time to be dressing your home at the moment. There is so much choice out there, you can create a really unique look in your home and stamp your style on your windows. Our aim is simply to help you take the idea in your mind and make it come to life on your windows".

Bespoke Blinds & Poles showcases one of the most comprehensive ranges of blinds, tracks and poles in the country. We specialise in solutions to bay and shaped windows, conservatory roofs, wet rooms, plus plantation shutters and motorised products.

www.sheffieldblinds.co.uk

follow us on Facebook
www.facebook.com/bespokeblindsandpoles

- **Blinds • Plantation Shutters • Awnings**
- **Conservatory Roof Specialists**
- **Curtain Poles • Curtain Tracks**
- **Bay Window Solutions**

6 Hutcliffe Wood Rd, Sheffield S8 0EX   0114 236 3100

187-191 Middlewood Rd, Hillsborough, Sheffield S6 4HD 0114 285384

Was that my teacher at Live Aid?

The Thompson Twins were always a bit different.
For starters, they were not twins. Mike Firth explains

Tom Bailey (right), one-time teacher at Brook School,
with fellow Twins Joe Leeway and Alannah Currie

WHICH band, formed in our area, performed at Live Aid in 1985, but not at Wembley Stadium?
It was the electro-poppers with the outrageous haircuts, The Thompson Twins, who sang at the Philadelphia leg of the 'Global Jukebox', being joined on stage by Madonna. It was all a mighty long way from the band's roots in Chesterfield and Sheffield where they had performed at venues including The Highfield pub at Newbold, The Broadfield on Abbeydale Road and The Big Tree at Woodseats.

For a couple of years from 1983, few groups in Britain were bigger than the Twins - named after the comical detectives in Hergé's Adventures of Tintin. Their success was mirrored across the Atlantic and one of their albums, 'Into The Gap', sold an astonishing five million copies worldwide.

So where did it all begin? Well, I first met the original Twins one lunchtime in 1978 when I nipped out of the newspaper office where I worked to buy a sandwich in Chesterfield town centre. Leaving the building at the same time as journalist colleague Pete Dodd, he asked if I'd rather call in at his house close to Saltergate football ground for a bite to eat. Food was actually the last thing on his mind; he and his band had a lunchtime rehearsal planned and I sat in on the practice session featuring Pete and colleagues John Roog, Tom Bailey and Jon Podgorski.

There were many towns and cities making great music in those days. Unfortunately Chesterfield wasn't one of them so after selling 1,500 copies of their debut single 'Squares and Triangle' in 1980, off they went to seek fame and fortune in London. At first the band expanded to seven members, then the line-up was slashed to just three. Sheffielder Bailey remained, together with Alannah Currie and Joe Leeway, and the trio created an eye-catching identity which was just as recognisable as their catchy lyrics.

The chart hits came thick and fast: 'Love On Your Side', 'We Are Detective', 'Hold Me Now' and the one later to be adopted by Sheffield Wednesday, 'You Take Me Up'. Another song, 'In The Name of Love', featured on the soundtrack of one of the era's most successful movies, 'Ghostbusters'.

Bailey, who had been a music and English teacher at Sheffield's Brook School for a short spell until 1977, was chiefly responsible for writing the Thompson Twins' songs, Currie played sax and was credited with perfecting the band's image and Leeway sang, wrote, played bongos and designed the stage shows.

The Live Aid gig should have been a platform for even greater things for the Twins but after Bailey suffered a breakdown, their successes dwindled and their 1991 album 'Queer' was the band's swansong.
• Do you remember seeing The Thompson Twins perform locally? Did Tom Bailey teach you at Brook School? Contact us at My Kind of Town.

Before the Thompson Twins became worldwide stars
they released this single locally which sold 1,500 copies

When fashion was on ration

The 1940s were the worst of times and the best of times for looking good. Mike Firth talks to two young women from Sheffield who are determined to keep classic styles from the era alive

All aboard for 40s fashion. Sheffield's Rachel and Alex Dean find the perfect setting to show off their 60-year-old outfits at Crich Tramway Village

SISTERS Rachel and Alex Dean have their gran to thank for sparking their passion for fashion - but it's not the latest high street trends the pair covet.

They simply adore turning back the clock to the 1940s, wearing authentic clothing which proves that the decade of "make do and mend" was also an era of style, grace and colour.

Rachel (26) and Alex (19) always knew that their gran Cathleen Dean had a large collection of 1940s clothing but only recently did they discover exactly how extensive it was. Now they all regularly attend celebrations of bygone days with fellow members of the UK Home Front organisation and scores of other enthusiasts.

The sisters, who grew up at Ecclesall and studied at Totley All Saints School, wear clothing, hats and

Three of a kind. Sheffield sisters Rachel (left) and Alex with their grandmother Cathleen
who lived through the 1940s and has a collection of many fabulous outfits from the era

shoes owned by Cathleen for 65 years or more, attending celebrations such as the 1940s weekends at Crich Tramway Museum in Derbyshire.

Explained Rachel: "Fashion in the 1940s was very elegant and girls could show off their figures without having to show too much skin. Women dressed as women and were very feminine with bright red lipstick and nails.

"It is amazing how brightly coloured the clothing and make-up was and when we dress up to attend events we know just how the pin-up girls of the era must have felt."

The pair say their gran's collection is all in pristine collection. She has kept wardrobes full of outfits, plus a vast range of coats, furs and accessories including 80 authentic hats and 39 pairs of original 1940s shoes. Some cardigans have been knitted in more recent years but always to patterns from 60 years ago.

World War II had a huge effect on fashion as clothes were in short supply and rationed. Older clothing was transformed into modern styles; pillowcases were turned into white shorts for summer and blankets were used to make warm winter coats.

With stockings being scarce, women ingeniously used gravy browning as leg make-up and asked friends to draw a straight line down the backs of their legs to give the impression that stockings were being worn.

After the war the austerity of the fashion world also came to an end and people celebrated peace by extravagantly dressing up and indulging themselves.

Rachel, who is training to be a teacher at Sheffield Hallam University, and Alex, currently studying performing arts and the media at The Birt School in London, say they enjoy helping to recapture the feeling and spirit of the 1940s when there was a genuine community spirit.

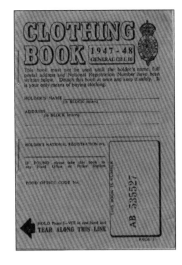

Explained Rachel: "We see ourselves as being something of a living memorial to people who were around in the 1940s. We enjoy wearing stylish clothing from those days but we also do it as a mark of respect."

Alex has an additional interest in attending festivals of bygone days as her boyfriend Jack Harris from Nottingham owns three historic vehicles plus a couple of anti-aircraft guns!

Added Cathleen: "When Alex and Rachel dress up and join me at events I am always the proudest person there.

"They remind me of myself when I was their age."

• Details of the UK Home Front organisation can be found at www.ukhomefront.co.uk

• Find out dates of future special events at Crich Tramway Museum in Derbyshire on www.tramway.co.uk

Alex and Rachel enjoy dressing up but also do it as a mark of respect for people who lived through our country's toughest decade

Memory store

In the days before supermarkets were invented, shopping in Sheffield was a completely different experience. Every suburb was well served by independent traders and the city centre had a variety of specialist shops. Some have survived but many have gone by the wayside. Do you recall any of these Sheffield businesses?

Before the H. Boldock family-run fish, game and poultry shop opened at Woodseats, there was this H. Boldock outlet at Attercliffe, opposite the bottom of Staniforth Road. The business had a near-miss in World War II when a bomb destroyed the shop next door.

My Kind of Shop

At one time Sheffield was full of corner shops and this one at the junction of Chesterfield Road and Little London Road was a beer-off come grocery store. Run by the Lee family in the 1930s and then the Eggo family from 1938 until 1951, it was well known for its green and cream tiles which were damaged during World War II. In more recent years this building was home to a car tyre business.

The name 'Mitchells' has been synonymous with Meadowhead for more than 75 years but what may surprise some readers is that the business has not always been an off-licence. It started out as a butcher's shop and this picture, taken in 1954, shows present proprietor John Mitchell, aged three, with his father, Frank Dennis Mitchell.

At one time, any Sheffielder wanting a new pet would have headed straight for Mace's. Did you get your family budgie here? Can you recall the tortoises which were kept in the window? Pictured here at the Exchange Street pet shop around 1982 are Harry Mace (left) and his assistant Chris Whitham. Sorry, we don't know the name of the snake but if we were asked to guess we would say he was called Monty

A schoolboy in war-torn Sheffield, Arthur Firth recalls how he enjoyed his days as an evacuee in the relative safety of the Nottinghamshire countryside

From Pitsmoor to Paradise

I WAS eight years and six months old when World War II was declared on September 3rd, 1939. Sheffield took part in the biggest evacuation this country has ever known and it must have been planned well in advance for the very next day hundreds of children and some parents with babies were waiting at Victoria Station for trains and buses to take them away from the city.

Some cities across Europe had already been bombed by the Nazis without warning and it was understandable that people here in Sheffield were so concerned. But what a worry it must have been for parents hoping they were sending their loved ones away to a safer place.

My parents, together with the mother of two brothers who were neighbours of ours, told us to stick together and look after each other in all difficulties. We were taken to Newark in Nottinghamshire but became separated from the main party when we got on the wrong bus.

We stayed in Newark for just one night, then went on to a little village called Balderton where we were the only evacuees to arrive. The three of us were put into a schoolroom until a lady arrived and said "I can take the two brothers." I was left with another lady and although we had not wanted to be split up, fortunately we found we were staying quite near each other.

Soon we were exploring the countryside, looking for rabbits and hares and gathering conkers. It was an entirely different life to the one we had left behind in Pitsmoor with the smoke and grime of the steelworks.

The couple I stayed with had no children of their own and treated me very well indeed. They took me cycling along the country lanes and we watched the farmers working in their fields of corn to gather the harvest.

It was so peaceful and quiet and there was no hint that there was a war on until one day, after the fall of Dunkirk, when hundreds of troops were camped in fields close to us. I gave one soldier a Mars Bar which I had bought with my pocket money for three pennies. In return he gave me a 2 Franc coin which I carried around with me for years afterwards.

The school we went to was close to the A1, known in those days as The Great North Road. There wasn't much normal traffic about in those days and although Army vehicles regularly travelled along it, you could cross it with ease.

When the air-raid siren sounded in school hours, the teacher let some children go home if they could run there in two or three minutes and if there was a parent there to meet them. Fortunately I only recall the siren sounding once and that was a practice run.

However, when I went home one day I walked across a field and looked to the sky where I could see planes shooting at each other. There were vapour-trails all over, but no siren had been sounded. The Germans were attacking our airfields before going on to bomb our cities. One night, when the siren sounded, the lady I was staying with put me under the stairs with my gas mask on for safety.

I joined the Cubs and made friends with some village lads of my own age. I remember one very hot day we were taken to an open-air swimming pool which was full. Two German planes flew right above us very low in the sky and we could see the crosses on their wings. Again no siren was sounded. They were probably spotter planes, mapping a course along the A1, for on March 7th, 1941, the Ransome and Marles factory in Newark was bombed with 41 people being killed.

Some weekends I returned to Pitsmoor, being put on a bus from Newark to Retford where I met my dad in Cannon Square and was then taken to Sheffield. I would return on Sunday evening, having always had a tale or two to tell my parents about the life I was living. I don't think they were too pleased about me being away from them.

Another wave of evacuees arrived in Balderton from London but I was only there for around 12 months before I sadly had to leave it all behind; the lovely house with its big garden and bathroom, the good pals I had made and the lovely couple who had taken care of me. My mother and dad paid them a visit to thank them for everything they had done for their son.

I had to return home to Sheffield because my dad's age group was next in line to receive their call-up papers and consequently my mother would have been left at home alone. So I returned to Pitsmoor from my life in the countryside and it took me a while to get used to things. My school had closed after suffering damage in a bombing raid, so children were being sent to a number of different schools.

Many evacuees returned home for one reason or another and although some had had a bad time of it, I had enjoyed my days as an evacuee and never regretted them.

Wanted: '70s movie stars

Did you enjoy fleeting fame as a movie star in 1970s Sheffield?
If you did, a team of documentary researchers may well want to talk to you

WERE you in the legendary Sheffield film that celebrates its 40th birthday this year? If so someone wants to hear from you.

ACM Retro are presently researching a documentary that explores the legacy of 'The Reel Monty' – the 1971 Sheffield film that ended being part of international hit movie 'The Full Monty'.

'The Reel Monty' captures the swinging city of the early 1970s like nothing else and took a full year to film. It includes footage of long-gone civic icons like the Hole In The Road; The Fiesta; the "streets in the sky" of the then ground-breaking Park Hill Flats complex; Sheffield Show in its heyday and Millhouses Park lido.

'The Reel Monty' would have been consigned to the archives if it wasn't for one of the most incredible stories in British movie history. In 1997 the makers of the flick were tracked down by a film company planning a low-budget movie about a bunch of redundant steelworkers turning to stripping for a living.

Jim and Marie-Luise Coulthard, who produced and directed the original film, pleased with the interest in their movie after all this time, gladly accepted the company's offer of £400 for the rights to use some of their footage.

By the time 'The Full Monty' received its fifth Oscar nomination, the couple had helped 20th Century Fox gross more than £180million!

The documentary is set to be included on a special 40th anniversary edition DVD of 'The Reel Monty'.

ACM Retro are also on the look out for any other 1970s cinefootage of Sheffield for the project. Please get in touch if you have anything.

If you have details of anyone in the film/cinefootage of Sheffield in the 1970s, either email this magazine at mike@heronpublications.co.uk or info@acmretro.com. You can also call 0845 603 6421.

Gone but not forg
plans are afoot t
the 20th anni
of the clo
Sheffield's f
Limit

Can you recall
seeing bands such
as The Photos
perform at West
Street's most
famous venue?

My Kind of Club

Pictures: Pete F

50

No Limit to city venue's appeal

Paul Young and Q-Tips on stage at The Limit

WHEN West Street's legendary Limit venue shut its doors for the last time in 1991, people thought it was the end of an era.

Few clubs had left such an indelible mark on Sheffield's after-dark scene or weathered so many tastes and changes over its 13 year reign.

"I think that's why I found the subject matter so interesting," said former Limit-goer Neil Anderson who penned 'Take It To The Limit' about the club.

"Everyone of a certain age in the region seemed to have a tale to recount about The Limit. The more people I spoke to, the more fascinated I became."

The book has been the catalyst for a breed of new Limit nights with former club-goers making contact for the first time in decades. In November 2011, a special event is set to take place to mark the 20th anniversary of the passing of the club.

The Limit was Sheffield's answer to The Hacienda but whilst its Lancashire counterpart famously lost a fortune, The Limit became a major financial success and even bankrolled the transformation of the Lyceum Theatre into a music venue in the early 1980s.

The West Street venue was originally opened by Sheffield favourites Bitter Suite.

The Limit's main aim was to give a home to the region's punk rockers and the likes of Siouxsie and the Banshees, Adam and the Ants, Generation X, Rezillos, Skids, Punishment of Luxury, Chelsea, Cockney Rejects, UK Subs, Ruts, Undertones, Dickies and scores more were soon gracing the stage.

But whilst the club was promoting punk bands from out of town, it also became pivotal to Sheffield's electro revolution of the early '80s, staging seminal gigs by the likes of Human League, Cabaret Voltaire, Comsat Angels and Vice Versa (who went on to become ABC).

Siouxsie Soux

The venue was a true one-off. It helped break bands that went onto national and international domination – everyone from U2 to B-52s played landmark shows there.

Neil Anderson said: "The Limit was untouched by the Winter of Discontent, the early '80s recession and the miners' strike and went on to host 13 years of club nights from early punk, mid-80s goth to early rave and dance."

"Take It To The Limit" was such a success local branches of Waterstones had sold out within 48 hours of the book going on sale. The book's launch party attracted a crowd of more than 700 with members of Sheffield bands Pulp, Human League, Vice Versa/ABC, Artery, Stunt Kites, The Extras and The Push in attendance.

Artist Paul Staveley has also immortalised some of the venue's most iconic gigs as part of the celebrations.

• More book, 20th anniversary event and painting information at www.takeittothelimit.info You can also join the 'Take It To The Limit' Facebook group.

Famous faces

Celebrities have always loved being pictured with Sheffield area folk - and here's the proof

In March 1959, shop owner Jeff Blackburn, seen here with singing star Alma Cogan, opened his new electrical shop in Chesterfield and invited the popular recording artist to cut the ribbon. Unfortunately, due to Alma's magnitude, the ceremony attracted hundreds of people and literally stopped all the traffic in Chesterfield town centre. Following the event, Alma was whisked back to Sheffield where she was topping the bill at The Empire.

Seen here in 1968 with the legendary Johnny Cash is the late Sheffield DJ Gaspin' Gus. This photograph was taken up in Carlisle to where Gus had travelled with Johnny on his tour bus.

Back in the 1970s there was no bigger star on TV than Dick Emery whose Saturday night shows pulled in millions of viewers. Can you remember the catchphrases? Here is Dick pictured with fans at the opening of the Sheaf Motors filling station and car showroom at Coal Aston.

Here's John Firminger coercing the great Bo Diddley to have his photograph taken with him backstage when the R&B legend played at Dingwalls in Sheffield in March, 1983.

Two members of Sheffield band The Hillbilly Cats, Graham Sargent and John Riley, pictured here with their hero, the 'Godfather of Rockabilly', Carl Perkins, backstage in Manchester in 1968

Have you ever been photographed with anyone famous? Send us your picture to share with other 'My Kind of Town' readers.

Do you recognise any of these budding young Sheffield cricketers? How about the smart looking boy wearing a tie on the far right of the back row? Does his dimpled face ring any bells?
This was Birkdale School's unbeaten cricket team of 1956, with team scorer none other than their most famous old boy, Monty Python's Michael Palin. He went on to travel the world but left his cricket bag at home.

Author Ann Sapcote (left) with three of the people who helped with the book, from left: Rev Steve Millwood, Alan Baggaley and Hazel Newton. They are standing outside Attercliffe Common's historic Hill Top Chapel that appears on the front of the book

Cliffe faces

Attercliffe Common's boom years have been brought back to life in a brand new book full of vivid memories and poignant pictures

FOR generations it was the beating heart of Sheffield's thriving East End. Attercliffe Common was home to the loyal workforce that kept local engineering giants like Brown Bayley and British Steel in production even through the Sheffield Blitz in 1940 that saw homes and industry in the area obliterated by two nights of devastating German attack.

But the demise of the city's heavy industrial sector in the 1970s not only signalled the death knell for thousands of jobs, it also heralded the end for one of the most concentrated and close-knit working class communities the city has ever known as bulldozers lined up to demolish thousands of homes in the name of progress.

Ann Sapcote's new book, 'My Family And Other Morticians', is a rare and poignant insight into the last great decade of Attercliffe Common in the 1960s.

Three years in the writing and researching, the publication contains scores of interviews with former residents, rare photos and a fascinating directory of the actual streets in question together with a house-by-house list of the names of the people that lived there.

Ann Sapcote is acutely aware there's little physical evidence left of the proud community that once lived there – Don Valley Bowl now occupies the site of her former home and the streets she

played in as a child.

She said: "The 1960s were the twilight years for Attercliffe Common and its population but none of us knew it at the time. Businesses were thriving, we had everything we needed on our doorstep and the post-war austerity years were fading into memory.

"I'm in debt to so many former residents who've been kind enough to relay their tales of humour, sadness and every day lives.

"Though it has been a fascinating journey to complete 'My Family And Other Morticians', I will, like thousands of others, never understand the kind of logic that destroys a whole community in the blink of an eye.

"The bustling Attercliffe captured in the book with its up market department stores like Banners and popular cinemas like the Adelphi is a far cry from the seedy, soulless suburb that exists today."

No-one has done more to keep the former community of Attercliffe Common together than Ann Sapcote.

She organises reunions for scores of ex-residents, produces a regular newsletters and had her first book on the area, 'Once Round The Lump', published in 2006.

Whilst the majority of her new book centres on the area's halcyon years of the 1960s, her journey of discovery starts as far back as the 17th century, before giving graphic accounts of a Victorian cholera outbreak and the draconian ways the powers that be dealt with the people of the area.

From farming community to the industrial heartland of Sheffield, Ann Sapcote leaves no stone unturned.

'My Family And Other Morticians' is published by ACM Retro and sells for £13.95. It is available from all good bookshops.

• Attercliffe's lost pubs - page 66

COLE BROS. F.C.

Cigarette packets scare us with their stark Government Health Warnings, but once they contained pictures of footballers and cricketers which were avidly collected by children. Mike Firth reports

History on the cards

S. & E. CO-OP SPORTS F.C.

L ONG before Panini temped young football fans with their colourful sticker collections of Premiership and World Cup stars, football fans collected pictures of their favourite footballers on cigarette cards.

Open a packet of fags and out would drop a picture of Ellis Rimmer (Wednesday), Ernest Needham (United) or any other star player of the 1920s or 1930s.

A piece of card had initially been included with cigarettes simply to protect them from being squashed. Companies such as W.D. & H.O. Wills soon realised the potential of this, producing a set of 50 pictures of famous cricketers in 1896.

Football was booming and in 1902 Wills published their first 66 football cards. This included George Hedley and Ernest Needham of United and Fred Spiksley from Wednesday.

Soon almost all tobacco companies were offering collectable cards, hoping to build up loyalty from their customers. Many of the football cards ended up in the hands of children. Could you imagine the outcry if such a marketing campaign were to be suggested today?

Writer Clifford Hough, pointed out that cigarette cards were dubbed "The Working Man's Encyclopedia" because they brought pictures of famous faces and fascinating places to the attention of the masses.

Ardath Tobacco Company did not issue cards until just before the First World War. Their first sets were reproductions of famous paintings by Rembrandt, Rubens , Raphael and Valasquez but in 1934 the company turned its attention to footballers.

It issued photocards of hundreds of football clubs from the famous to the not-so-famous. In the latter category were the local line-ups on this page from a 1936 collection of 110 Yorkshire football teams.

It's unlikely that many of these footballers from the Co-op, Cole Bros, Bankers, Police or Teachers will still be around, but look closely and you may recognise your father or grandfather. We would be delighted to hear from you if you do.

SHEFFIELD BANKERS F.C.

SHEFFIELD TEACHERS F.C.

SHEFFIELD CITY POLICE F.C.

The Power of Love

Chris and Ann on their wedding day in 1977

A 1970s photo discovery provided the spark to relight romance for a Sheffield couple - and it's even better than before!

WHEN Ann and Chris Jackson went their separate ways over a quarter-of-a-century ago it definitely marked the end of an era, or so they thought...

Their love originally blossomed in 1970s Sheffield and much of their courting took place in long-gone venues like Eyre Street's Hofbrauhaus venue, The Fiesta and the Penny Farthing nightspot.

They even had their wedding reception in Hofbrauhaus in 1977 where Sheffield-born Ann worked as a barmaid. But by the 1980s their relationship had gone the same way as the stack heels of the era before and Chris remained in his native Wrexham where the couple had set up home whilst Ann moved back to Sheffield.

Ann, who was just 17 years old when she began dating Chris, said: "It wasn't as though Chris had done anything wrong – we just never saw one another because he was working the entire time helping to run the family haulage business."

Though she ended up remarrying and having two children, she freely admits nothing could ever match the excitement of her time in 1970s Sheffield with her first love.

But little did she know that life was about to take a bizarre twist of fate that would put her back in the arms of her first love and transport her back to the very heart of life - 1970s Sheffield.

Local author Neil Anderson spent a full year researching his 'Dirty Stop Out's Guide to 1970s Sheffield' book which was published last year and admits one of his favourite photos in the whole book was one of a wedding party sat in the Hofbrauhaus venue (which was then known as the Bierkeller).

He said: "I amassed literally hundreds of photos in my research but only had room for a small fraction. One particular one caught my eye straight way; it was of a bride and groom looking totally made for each other."

Ann, now 54 years old and still living in Sheffield, was shocked when she heard of the photo's re-emergence in the book 33 years after it was taken.

She said: "A car suddenly screeched to halt when I was walking to the bus stop and my friend Jacqueline, who also used to work at the Hofbrauhaus with her husband Orrett, shouted out 'I've just seen you in this new book on your wedding day!'"

News of its appearance soon reached the ears of Chris in Wales who didn't need much persuading to attend the book's launch party – a '70s reunion night in Sheffield city centre held in October 2010. The most important reunion that night turned out to be Ann and

Let's Get Together Again... Chris and Ann reunited in 2011

Chris who'd not seen each other for 26 years.

Neil Anderson's timing for the publication couldn't have been better.

Ann had got divorced two years earlier and Chris, now 60, was also single; it seemed nothing had really come close to what they had all those years earlier.

Ann said: "He told me he'd only ever had one love and had sworn never to marry again. He kept that promise until he asked me to marry him – again!"

Guests travelled from as far away as Switzerland for their second wedding that took place at Sheffield's glitzy Rutland Hotel in April this year.

Neil Anderson, author of the 'Dirty Stop Out's Guide to 1970s Sheffield' and the man responsible for love second time around, said: "It has been a real honour to have been the person that has set this amazing chain of events in motion."

And what do Ann's kids - Joshua, 20, and Ellie, 14 - think of their mother's impending nuptials?

Ann said: "The only thing they ever had a problem with was the fact Chris now looks smaller than he did in the '70s. That can be explained easily – he doesn't wear platforms anymore!"

• More info on the book from www.acmretro.com

Jewel of a business for almost

100 years

ESTABLISHED at Woodseats for more than 95 years, D. W. Garrett Jewellers prides itself on traditional values like friendly, professional service and honest prices.

Owner David has more than 30 years experience in the industry and can help with all of your jewellery-related queries, from altering ring sizes and putting new clasps on necklaces to replacing watch batteries.

With gold prices at an all-time high, customers also appreciate David's expert advice when it comes to exchanging their unwanted gold for cash.

"People often don't know what they've got, which is why I say to people just bring it in and I'll go through it," explained David.

"You can miss a lot If you don't know what you're doing. I don't care what it is and if it's not my field, I'll find someone to pass it on to.

"You don't need a lot to make a lot. You never know what you're going to get offered. I always say the best thing to do is come in because sometimes things are worth more as an article than they are as scrap."

People often don't realise how much they've acquired over the years until they start looking and many a happy customer has left Garrett

pleasantly surprised with how much their 'junk' was actually worth.

Aware that not everyone can get along to the Chesterfield Road shop easily, anyone housebound is welcome to call David and make an appointment for him to visit them at home.

Almost a century old and one of the area's oldest businesses, David added: "For as long as anyone can remember there has been a Garrett's jewellery shop here and for generations of local families it is something of an institution.

"They like the friendly, helpful service we offer and they also appreciate our prices which are generally a good deal cheaper than you would pay in the larger jewellery stores."

Whether you're looking for jewellery, a stylish watch or a clock, if D. W. Garrett doesn't have what you're looking for in stock, they can usually find it in a few days.

D.W. Garrett Jewellers is open Monday to Saturday from 9am to 5.30pm at 724 Chesterfield Road, Woodseats, Sheffield 8. Tel 0114 255 4814

Sheffield - City

Colourful poster promoting 'The Case of Charles Peace'

Few people growing up in Sheffield would ever think of themselves as living on a movie set, but many films have been made in and around the city. John Firminger recalls the blockbusters and those movies which are not so well known

George Baker and Diana Dors in 'Tread Softly Stranger'

WHEN I was a lad growing on the Arbourthorne, I'd never have imagined Sheffield as a prime location to make films. Hollywood? yes, Paris? yes, London? yes, Sheffield? eh?

Even when we played cowboys and Indians in nearby Buck Woods, our imagination would take us to some other place far away where the surroundings were wilder and more akin to our fantasies. Although I loved it dearly (and still do), I just hadn't seen Sheffield as a place to make films. Maybe because I'd taken it for granted whilst I was busy growing up and subsequently getting sidetracked by other things such as going to work and having a family and never really appreciated its finer points till later in life?

Like many things, it took someone from outside the city to have the vision and foresight to see it as an ideal place to use in films. Was this due to its industrial history, its hilly terrain, the attitude and directness of the people, or just its northern ambience?

Of course the city had already been recognised by the entertainment industry for its contribution to music and sport. Maybe it was some of this that also sparked off some interest from the film industry? Whatever it was, it was indeed good to see Sheffield receive some further and well-deserved attention and over the years there have been a number of films made in and around the city, adding further to its credentials.

We celebrate the fact by way of a run-down of films connected with Sheffield and neighbouring areas.

The Case of Charles Peace (1949)

Although not made in Sheffield, its subject matter has, of course, strong ties with the city. Written by Doris Davison and Norman Lee, this is a full-length film adaptation of the notorious Victorian burglar-turned-murderer.

Barrister, St. Clement Barnes KC played by Valentine Dyal, delivers a lecture to police recruits, relating the story of Victorian murderer Charles Peace who changed identity to elude the cops. Leading a double-life, by day he was a respected local businessman but had a quick and nasty temper that would only occasionally show through his more civilised persona during the day.

With Michael Martin Harvey as Charles Peace, Former silent film star Chili Bouchier as Kathryn Dyson, Richard Shane as Arthur Dyson, well known British film actor Ronald Adam in the role of Defence Council Lockwood and Bruce Belfrage as Prosecution Council Foster.

As a professional thief at night Charlie Peace raided houses in various northern cities including Sheffield. For a time he was known to live in Britannia Road, Darnall. Peace was an expert cat burglar and would make his escape by scurrying over neighbourhood rooftops.

It's quite amusing to see how Darnall is depicted in this film as a quiet country village (which it was at the time) with the Dysons first living in Britannia Cottages, before moving across town to Banner Cross where Peace continued to pursue Kathryn Dyson and subsequently murdered Arthur Dyson.

Under the name of John Ward, Peace continued to operate in the south of England before more murderous acts brought about his ultimate demise.

Tread Softly Stranger (1957)

This tense film Noir is about two brothers, one of whom, Johnny Mansell is on the run from a London gang after owing them a lot of money, whilst his brother Dave is a lowly wages clerk working at a northern steelworks.

His girlfriend is the sultry blonde nightclub hostess Calico for whom he's embezzled £300 in order to keep her affections. The three plan a wages robbery to repay Dave's fraud and Johnny's debts. Unfortunately their plans go wrong and a murder ensues.

Starring Diana Dors, George Baker, Terence Morgan, Russell Napier, Wilfred Lawson and Patrick Allen. Set in the fictional town of Rawborough and filmed in the Parkgate area of Rotherham, where it was shot most effectively in black and white, adding to the film's tense storyline.

The railway station where George Baker arrives at near the start is the Parkgate & Rawmarsh station. Parkgate had a big steelworks which was identifiable from the two blast furnaces. The nightime scene in the film when Terence Morgan and George Baker "break" into the steelworks and the internal scene featuring Patrick Allen were filmed at the Phoenix Works (Steel, Peech & Tozer) of United Steel at Templeborough. (Available on DVD).

in the Movies

Comedy great Nat Jackley appeared in the harrowing 'Threads'

The Moor, Sheffield, in '69, as seen in 'City on the Move'

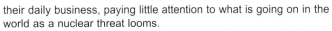

Sheffield: City on the Move (1969)

In 1969, Sheffield City Council took on its first ever publicity officer, a man called Peter Wigley. It is he who can be credited with the idea for this film, a promotional documentary looking at Sheffield and its 'boom and bust' era with the steel industry still managing to stay at the forefront. It featured plenty of local footage and was produced and directed by Jim and Marie-Luise Coulthard.

Sheffield is also seen as a 'swinging city', basking in the success of tourism and commerce. The film boasts long-gone icons like the Hole in the Road (an award-winning subterranean, pedestrianised area with shops, tropical fish tank and all-weather escalators). Other footage shows the Sheffield Show in its heyday, Millhouses Park lido and the Park Hill Flats, dubbed 'streets in the sky.' At The Fiesta nightclub (the biggest in Europe at the time) we see various performers including Bob Monkhouse and Matt Monro.

F.I.S.T. (1978)

Sylvester Stallone appeared in this US-made film about trade union leaders in America. Johnny Kovak (Stallone) joins the Teamsters trade-union in a local chapter in the 1930s and works his way up in the organisation. As he climbs higher, his methods become more ruthless and finally Senator Madison (Rod Steiger) campaigns to find the truth about the alleged connections with the Mob.

Most of the film was shot in Dubuque, Iowa, USA, but for some reason, parts of this film were done in Sheffield, probably due to its industrial background. Directed by Norman Jewison, it had a great cast with Boyle, Melinda Dillon, Brian Dennehy, and a young Anthony Kiedis (Flea from the Red Hot Chili Peppers). (Available on DVD).

Threads (1984)

Harrowing documentary-style account set in the mid-80s of a nuclear holocaust and how it affects the working class city of Sheffield and the eventual long-run effects of nuclear war on civilization.

Sheffield couple Ruth Beckett (Karen Meagher) & Jimmy Kemp (Reece Dinsdale) are planning for their forthcoming marriage and birth of their first child. The families of Ruth and Jimmy go about their daily business, paying little attention to what is going on in the world as a nuclear threat looms.

One spring day, without warning, the Soviet Union attacks the United Kingdom with ICBMs - two of which hit Sheffield, annihilating most of the city and its inhabitants. But what is even more horrifying is the aftermath - a world without public order, clean food, water, electricity, or the ability to produce any of them.

Ruth struggles for more than ten years just to stay alive in this horrible, barren, radioactive homeland.

Footage of Sheffield sees some impressive effects and its quite alarming to see parts of the city centre, including the 'Egg-Box' getting obliterated in the attacks.

Filming was done in and around Sheffield and seen were the Nottingham House pub in Broomhill, RAF Finningley, Doncaster, Curbar Edge and in Derbyshire.

The Bunker seen in the film was in the basement of Sheffield Town in Pinstone Street.

With its realism, this is a film that Sheffielders probably find most uncomfortable. Amongst those spotted in cast were comedian Ted Beyer, veteran comic Nat Jackley and actors Patrick Allen and Leslie Judd. (Available on DVD).

I.D. (1994)

Tough and violent movie made by BBC Films about four police officers who go undercover to infiltrate a hooligan firm that supports the fictional football club Shadwell Town FC, in order to discover the identity of the ringleader. However, as the officers are drawn into the macho world of hard drinking and frequent violence, John (played by Reece Dinsdale) soon finds himself turning into one of the thugs that he was originally sent to investigate.

The other three officers are able to keep some perspective on their relationship with Shadwell and its fans whilst John gets further involved and ends up stabbing a rival fan. By the end of the film he's seen joining in a neo-Nazi march in the same way he embraced the lifestyle of a football hooligan, although maybe he is still under-cover?

Featuring some pretty unsavoury characters and including Warren Clarke and Sean Pertwee in the cast. Whilst the film is supposed to

Shadwell supporters in the centre of Rotherham in the 1994 film 'I.D.'

Sheffield movie star in a Sheffield film, 'When Saturday Comes'

The biggest blockbuster of them all, 'The Full Monty'

be situated in the south, in the fictional area of Shadwell, some of the outside filming took place in Sheffield (Midland Station) and mainly around the centre of Rotherham, including the Market and Millmoor Football ground. (Available on DVD).

When Saturday Comes (1996)

The first film to actually feature Sheffield in its own right, about brewery worker and heavy drinker Jimmy Muir who also unfortunately has an arrogant lack of respect for any kind of authority.

His entire life has been centred around football with which he certainly shows potential, but has never had the courage or discipline to make anything of it. Playing for his local pub team, Jimmy is spotted by Ken Jackson, the scout for the local non-league Hallam football club.

With the club, Jimmy's playing ability is constantly brilliant and Ken puts his name forward for a trial at Sheffield United. Unfortunately the evening before the trial Jimmy gets drunk and wakes up feeling very rough. Consequently he fails to impress the Sheffield United manager.

Jimmy then has to consider his future, his choices and if he has the self-discipline to succeed. Playing the role, Sean Bean actually fulfilled a personal ambition when he played football for United at Bramall Lane. A penalty-taking scene was filmed in front of the kop at half-time of a Sheffield United v Manchester United fixture. United legend Tony Currie appears in the movie.

With plenty of local footage, although the eagle-eyed will notice that some of the continuity is a bit awry as we see Jimmy and his mates enter The Wentworth House pub in Attercliffe but the interior shots were filmed several miles away inside the John O'Gaunt pub at Gleadless Valley! (Available on DVD).

Reece Dinsdale

The Full Monty (1997)

This highly-acclaimed award winner is what really brought Sheffield world fame. Portraying a bunch of unemployed local men who see no hope of any work in the future. Sparked off by the success of male stripping groups such as the Chippendales, they decide to follow suit, in a tongue-in-cheek attempt to make some money.

Starring Robert Carlisle and Tom Wilkinson with an excellent supporting cast, all of whom enjoyed further success and recognition as a result of their appearance in this film.

However the film's highlights are the many familiar locations around Sheffield such as Parkwood Springs, Neepsend, Page Hall, The Shiregreen Club, etc.

Part of the documentary 'City On The Move' is featured at the beginning of the film, although set against the theme of the film, it should may have been retitled 'City At A Standstill'. Jim and Marie-Luise Coulthard were pleased with the interest in their film after all this time, and accepted their £400 offer for the rights to use some of the footage. By the time The Full Monty received its fifth Oscar nomination, the couple had helped 20th Century Fox gross over £180 million!

As a result of the film's success, the city saw a number of businesses exploiting it such as the Shiregreen Club, the Full Monty Café and the Full Monty Guided Tour - and why not? (Available on DVD)

Amongst Giants (1998)

Perhaps hoping to catch some of the attention afforded to The Full Monty, this film is let down by the slow moving story line.

The late Pete Postlethwaite is in charge of a gang painting pylons out on the moors outside Sheffield. The gang are struggling to make the job pay and are also up against a time limit before the

Pete Postlethwaite, Rachel Griffiths and James Thornton outside the Fox & Duck at Tinsley during the making of 'Amongst Giants'

'Whatever Happened to Harold Smith?' actors James Corden and Michael Legge walking down Hawley Street

Joe Absolom and Kelly Harrison in 'Dream'

power is switched back on again! Adding to their problems, Pete also falls in love with young female traveller (Rachel Griffiths) who joins the gang.

Included in cast are Lennie James (Snatch), Andy Zerkis (Sex, Drugs & Rock'n'Roll) and James Thornton (Emmerdale).

The storyline is a bit over the top in places but the film is worth watching for the various locations such as outside the Fox & Duck, Tinsley, inside The Vine, Cemetery Road, on top of the Gas Tower in Neepsend, underneath one of the Twin Towers, Tinsley, and the Nether Edge/Abbeydale area where Pete's in temporary accommodation.

When the gang attends a country music night at a local club, playing onstage is the Doncaster band Big Sky who include Sheffield musicians Steve 'Bubbles' Mitchell (drums) and Patrick Walker (fiddle). (Available on DVD).

Whatever Happened to Harold Smith? (2001)

The story revolves around 18-year-old Vince Smith (Michael Legge) who has a ongoing attraction to the music of Saturday Night Fever and goes into a Travolta pose at the drop of a hat.

Set in the 70s, his job is only just bearable due to his colleague Joanna who he constantly flirts with. His Mother Irene is something of a floozy whilst his stay-at-home Dad, Harold, has somehow acquired some telekinetic powers with which he can levitate himself. Unfortunately, whilst demonstrating this he stops all the pacemakers at an old folk's home!

After his confusion of seeing Joanna with a group of local punks, Vince manages to combine the fashion with his musical tastes and wins Joanna over.

Starring the great Tom Courtney as Harold Smith, Lulu as Vince's mother and Laura Fraser as Joanna Robinson. The cast also includes Stephen Fry, David Thewlis, James Corden (with a northern accent!) and Keith Chegwin.

Although set in a fictional northern town, the film was made in Sheffield and features plenty of footage in such locations as Campo Lane, Hawley Street and Blast Lane. Disco scenes

were also filmed at the disused Leadmill Road Bus Depot and the Adelphi, Attercliffe. (Available on DVD).

Dream (2001)

Cult film (has its own fan-club) apparently filmed in Stocksbridge and starring Joe Absolom (Doc Martin) and Kelly Harrison (Casualty).

The story is about a 'local lass' hairdresser who gets pregnant to her boyfriend and then wins a fashion competition arranged by this sleazy fashion/TV star. Following her dream of being a model, she goes down to London and makes it big. Things of course go all wrong and the girl's father and boyfriend both go after her and a happy ending ensues.

Produced 'as a successor to The Full Monty' but unfortunately it never found any distributors in this country and was released 'Down Under'. Also featuring Brian Conley, Sinead Cusack and Patrick Mower among the cast.

Some of the familiar scenes in and around Stocksbridge are the hairdressers at the top of Victoria Road, McKintyre Road near Alpine Lodge, the Victory Club plus views of the village from across the valley. Sheffield Speedway at Owlerton Stadium is also featured.

Women In Love (1969)

Ken Russell's, at times, sensational adaptation of D.H. Lawrence's story about love, sex and relationships in middle-class Victorian England, starring Glenda Jackson, Jennie Linden, Oliver Reed and Alan Bates.

The filming took place in Derbyshire, Nottinghamshire, Yorkshire, Northumberland, County Durham and Switzerland. The Derbyshire scenes were shot in Matlock, and in Sheffield the school scenes were filmed at Newhall Junior School, Sanderson Street, Brightside, which was demolished over 25 years ago.

• Next issue: John Firminger tunes in to watch Sheffield on the Box!

ONE man's mission to locate a missing chapter of Sheffield RSPCA's proud history has enjoyed a happy conclusion... with a little help from the publishers of this magazine and workers in faraway China.

Call in at the local charity's splendid new Animal Centre at Woodbourn Road, Attercliffe, and you will find state-of-the-art facilities and all manner of creature comforts. Right in the middle of the complex, however, is a striking item from a bygone era.

Way back in 1892, when Sheffielders relied upon horse-drawn transport to get around, an 8ft long drinking trough was placed in Fitzalan Square to offer refreshment for the overworked nags. It was dedicated to the work of Benjamin Cartledge who had been a

veterinary surgeon with the Sheffield Society for the Prevention of Cruelty to Animals for 20 years.

The engraved trough, made by the North of Scotland Granite Company of red Peterhead granite and costing £120, can be seen on some old photographs of Fitzalan Square. Peterhead granite was said to be "the best and finest in Scotland and it admits of a very high polish."

It is understood that the horse trough was repositioned in Barkers Pool in 1912 but when the War Memorial and City Hall were built there in the 1920s and 30s, it disappeared.

RSPCA trustee and historian Pete Smith spent four years trying to track down the huge trough's whereabouts, carrying out an

Tale of the trough

Mike Firth recounts the remarkable story of a historic Sheffield horse trough (pictured left) which vanished for more than 80 years... only to reappear right on cue

exhaustive search of Sheffield Archives, City Library documents, old newspapers and Town Hall departments. Several people assisted him, but to no avail. The trough had vanished.

Finally, Pete wrote to Active8, a local magazine produced by the publishers of 'My Kind of Town', to enquire whether any reader had information.

Said Pete at the time: "I would be eternally grateful to hear from anyone, even if it is bad news. It could be that it might have been smashed up and put under a motorway somewhere but at least I will be able to stop searching."

However, a couple of people did contact Pete through the magazine and the news on the trough's whereabouts was distinctly positive.

Two of the magazine's readers, Anthea Nicol and Stephen Tunnard, suggested that Pete should visit the city's Abbeydale Industrial Hamlet, but having previously been told by museum staff that there was no trough there, he was not particularly hopeful.

However, when Anthea pinpointed the exact spot where she believed she had seen a pink trough peeping up through thick undergrowth at the Hamlet, Pete thought it would be worthwhile making a return visit to Abbeydale Road South.

And hey presto... the size of the trough and the inscription around its rim left Pete in no doubt at all that this was what he had been searching for for four years.

"I was like a kid at Christmas," he said. "To find it after such a long time and in such good condition was amazing."

Equally astonishing was the timing of the discovery. After being missing for more than eight decades, it had reappeared just as the local RSPCA was preparing to move to its brand new home from their old Spring Street premises.

Said Pete: "Goodness knows where it had been through all those years but I was thrilled to bits to have found it."

The trough was transported across the city to be sited in a memorial garden at the Animal Centre... but there was still one big problem. Although the trough was in excellent condition, its eight granite legs had gone walkabout.

A stonemason gave the charity a quotation of £8,000 to provide replacement granite legs but that was way too much to spend.

Explained trustee Pete: "We tried to get a 100% Heritage Lottery Grant but we would have had to jump through so many hoops. We couldn't justify spending so much money when we have to raise funds to keep the centre going so I thought we were going to be stuck."

The Sheffield branch of the RSPCA doesn't receive money from the central RSPCA organisation and so relies on donations and local fund-raising to keep the centre running and hundreds of animals well cared for.

Luckily, businesswoman Hailin Williams, of Rotherham, heard the tale of the trough and organised for the replacement legs to be made in China, with Sheffield RSPCA only paying for the cost of materials and delivery, which came to just £50 per leg.

Hailin, whose husband is an artist, explained: "The legs were made in part of south-east China where stone is one of the major industries. They produce all kinds of stone projects, like memorials.

"I was already aware of the work of the local RSPCA because we originally adopted our dog Bobby from there."

Hailin first became known to the Animal Centre when she donated a large stone dog figurine, which was a memorial to Bobby. It was suggested to Pete that he should contact Hailin to see if she might be able to help.

Added Pete: "When the legs arrived and we put them on, I couldn't believe the similarity to how the original ones would have been. I felt very proud, to be honest, and so did one of our volunteers Gordon Brookfield, because we had both put in such a huge amount of work."

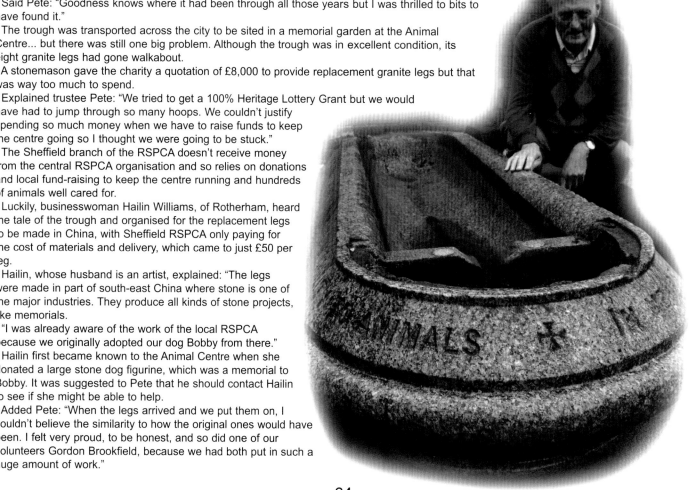

Left: Sheffield RSPCA Trustee Pete Smith finally locates the horse trough in thick undergrowth at Abbeydale Industrial Hamlet

Below left: Pete inspects the trough on its arrival at the Animal Centre at Attercliffe

Below: The eight replacement legs in the factory in China

Bottom: The trough goes on display at the new Animal Centre with, from left: RSPCA volunteer Gordon Brookfield, businesswoman Hailin Williams, Pete Smith and RSPCA chair Kathryn Whitlam

Attercliffe pub crawl

Michael Liversidge, author and local historian, takes us on a nostalgic drinking tour of Sheffield's East End pubs

The Pheasant Inn is now an Indian restaurant

MORE than 30 public houses were situated alongside the main Attercliffe Common and Attercliffe Road thoroughfare which ran from Weedon Street, for about one-and-a-half miles, up to its junction with Savile Street close to the Wicker Arches.

The **Commercial** (technically not on Attercliffe Common, but near enough) was followed by **The Royal Hotel**, **The Union**, **Carbrook Hall**, **Pheasant Inn**, **Excelsior**, **Broughton Inn**, **Lambpool**, **Filesmiths**, **Amberley Hotel**, **Salutation**, **The Gate**, **Hill Top Hotel**, **Tramcar**, **Golden Ball**, **Greyhound**, **Travellers Inn**, **Omnibus**, **Coach and Horses**, **King's Head**, **Station Hotel** or **Inn** (it was called both in its time), **Queen's Head**, **Horse and Jockey**, **Victoria Hotel**, **Dog and Partridge**, **Carlton**, **Robin Hood**, **Sportsman**, **Green Dragon**, **Bulldog**, **Washford Arms**, **Norfolk Arms**, **Rawson**, **Old King John Hotel** and finishes at **The Old Twelve O'Clock**.

The **Rawson** and **Old King John Hotel** were long gone before my drinking days began in 1964, however I did have a drink in all the others, but only as a youngster in the **Victoria** and **Omnibus**.

The **Arena Square** and **Players Cafe** (Carbrook Elementary School) have been opened in the last 20 years or so. Sadly the Players Cafe struggled to survive and was closed a few years after its high profile opening.

If you veered just a tad off the 'Cliffe then there was the **Burns Hotel**, **Tinsley Hotel** and **Yellow Lion**.

On Carbrook Street and Dunlop Street you could visit the **White Lion**, **British Oak**, **New Inn**, **Industry**, and on Milford Street was the **Fitzwilliam** and **Wentworth** (still serving today).

On Broughton Lane you could enjoy a pint at the **Bird in Hand**, **Enfield**, and **Railway** (now the **Noose and Gibbett**) and head down Janson Street and Hawke Street to the **Wellington** and **Blucher**.

Up onto Tinsley Park Road there was **The Friendship** and **The Fisherman's Rest** and veer off onto Worksop Road where five more pubs awaited the discerning drinker: **Britannia**, **Cocked Hat**, **Cutlers**, **White Hart** and **Old Blue Bell** (now a mosque). Just under the aquaduct were the **Sportsman** and **Albert**.

Newhall Road housed another five pubs: **Vine Tavern**, **Forge**, **Lodge**, **Junction** and **Brickmakers Arms**.

Other nearby public houses, just a small detour off the upper 'Cliffe, were **The Staniforth Arms**, **The Albert**, **The Plumpers**, **Lowdrop**, **North Pole**, **Grey Horse** and **'Ole in t' Wall**.

I have probably missed quite a few, but I am sure, you, the eagle-eyed reader will point out my omissions.

Cheers!

The Salutation and the Pavilion Picture House are seen here with many more shops and businesses stretching along Attercliffe Common

when a pub used to be on every corner
Literature available detailing the disappearing Public Houses of Sheffield

In the late 1970s or early 1980s Wilf Banks, with the help of the Monteney Community Workshop, produced a book called **A Pub on Every Corner** (left). It was a blue cover A4 booklet with typewritten text and hand drawn maps, sadly, not all totally accurate.

It was a little masterpiece for which anyone with an interest in the history of Sheffield Public Houses should be eternally grateful. This book had no images but was full of maps with all the pubs Wilf could remember marked in situ.

Soon after Wilf died, in 1995, Douglas Lamb revamped the book and fleshed it out with pub images and historic facts and details. He still kept Wilf's original pub list and maps, although redrawn to suit the more discerning reader.

A Pub on Every Corner (left) was a 254 page, 8" x 10" book published by Hallamshire Press.

Around the same time Wilf Banks was producing his original book, a chap called Roy Davey published **Pubs & People around Sheffield** (left). This was an A5, yellow covered booklet with over 100 pages. Costing only £2 it was a very informative little gem. The book had about 20 to 30 images of old Sheffield Pubs.

In 1991 J. P. Turley produced a small book titled **Pictures of Lost Sheffield Pubs**. A little landscape booklet consisting of 68 pages with 50 images of old pubs and a small descriptive caption to each image.

This was published by Harry Good Limited a Sheffield Print company.

101 Pictures of Lost Sheffield Pubs, another little landscape booklet by J P Turley. The author used his original 50 images of old pubs and added another 51 pictures to give a nice booklet full of memory jogging photographs. A couple of these pubs are incorrectly captioned, so beware if using for historic reference.

Sheffield's Yesterdays, another booklet by J P Turley. The author, once again uses about 16 of his original old pubs images but adds plenty more photographs of old Sheffield

In 1999 **The Definitive A-Z of Sheffield Public Houses** by Michael Liversidge was produced by Pickard Publishing. This book is A4 sized with over 200 pages containing over 600 public house images. A very informative book.

Produced by Pickards Publishing (now renamed youbooks.co.uk)

In 2000 Douglas Lamb followed up his highly successful A Pub on Every Corner with **Last Orders** a book detailing the outlying public houses of Sheffield.

Villages: Grenoside, Stannington, Wortley, Greenhill etc are all featured in this excellent book produced by Pickard Publishing (now renamed youbooks.co.uk).

With over 200 images-filled pages this is a genuine collectors item as only 1000 were ever printed.

In 2007 Pickards (youbooks) followed up their highly successful A-Z of Sheffield Public Houses with **Time Gentlemen Please**. This is an unusual book in that it shows full colour images of pubs that have now all finished serving the Sheffield public.

An A4 Landscape book.

In 2008 as if not to be outdone, prolific Sheffield author, J R Wrigley produced **T'owd Locals**. This is an A5 landscape booklet with very old images of long forgotten Sheffield Hostelries.

A wonderful sepia toned piece of Sheffield public house history.

A new little A6 booklet titled **Cheers from the 'Cliffe** shows about 30 public houses that used to adorn the Attercliffe Common and Attercliffe Road thoroughfare.

The books shown in the left hand column are now out of print and probably best found on e-bay or old book shops.

The books in the right hand column can still be purchased at Sheffield Scene-Surrey St, Sheffield Star, Waterstones, WH Smiths or online at youbooks.co.uk

How many of these city pubs can you recall?

Mike Firth has a little fun with the names of some of Sheffield's older pubs

YOU can't beat a game of **Cricket Inn** summer beneath the **Sun**. The **Brickmakers** got changed in the **Woodman's Hut** by the **Riverside** and, using a bat made from a **Willow Tree** and a strange **Old Blue Ball**, they took on their friends the **Bricklayers** who were a team of real **Oddfellows**.

They walked through the **Gate** and a **Hole in the Wall**, onto the **Farfield**, and looked a real **Sportsman's Group**. **Cuthbert Bank** and **Tim Bobbin**, wearing **Harlequin** caps, opened the batting, **Douglas** and **Chantrey** were a pair of **Blacksmiths** who had left their **Anvil** to open the bowling and **Montgomery** and an **Old English Gentleman** called **Lord Ratcliffe** were umpires.

After the **Owd Shake Hands**, the game got underway at **Twelve O'Clock**, watched by **Victoria** and the **Prince of Wales** who was wearing an **Old Crown**.

Billy Lees hit the **Ball Inn** the air so high that it cleared the **Big Tree**, **Alma Cottage** and the **Church** before landing in the **Reservoir** where the **Anglers Rest**. The **Cricket Ball** disturbed a **Black Swan** which bit a **Brown Cow**, **Lion and Lamb**.

A **Durham Ox** was so startled that it trod on a **Bee Hive**, spoiling the afternoon for **Wadsley Jack** and a **Mermaid** who, with a **Merry Heart**, had been playing **Chequers Hand in Hand** beneath the **Cherry Tree**, close to the **Abbey**.

It was a real **Mad House**. A **Fat Cat** chased an **Owl**, **Pheasant**, **Peacock** and **Hen and Chickens** and it was **Little Wonder** that **Sir Robert Peel**, a **Blue Boy**, had to provide a **Strong Arm**. He threatened to bring the **Army Inn** if the offenders refused to **Live and Let Live** and raise the **Royal Standard**.

Another of the **Cricketers**, Albert, arrived late on the **Tramcar**, having missed the **Omnibus**. He was cold because he had **Norton**. He had already scored **Three Tuns** and was the **Star** of the team. He went out to bat after a hurried **Ploughman's** lunch of **Grapes** and **Cheshire Cheese** with a cup of **Earl Grey**, but he had spent too long with the **Brewer on the Bridge** and was soon a **Green Man** in the **Infirmary**.

His place was taken by a **Shepherd Inn** a **Deerstalker** who usually batted at **Number One**, but on this occasion was **Old Number Twelve**. He proved to be a real **Snake Inn** the grass, hitting one shot into a **Railway** waggon which disappeared beneath the **New Bridge** towards **Cambridge**.

Another big hit over **Local Fields** went so far that the umpire signalled a **Double Six** and presented him with the **Cup** and an **Old Tankard**.

The players left **The Park** and, after a **Bath**, headed for the **Vine Vaults** where they drank enough to quench the thirst of an **Elephant**. There is a picture in the **Museum**.

Do you have memories of a particular pub in Sheffield? Perhaps one which no longer exists? Write to us at My Kind of Town, 24 Hutcliffe Wood Road, Beauchief, Sheffield, S8 0EX.

Inn proved too popular

ONE of the saddest sights in Sheffield these days is the number of pubs which are boarded up. Many of them were extremely popular venues at one time and their demise would have been unthinkable to their thousands of former 'regulars'. However, our sister magazine 'Active8' was reminded that many years ago one pub closed because it proved *too popular*! Nick Williams of Norton sent us the following account:

In 1830 Sheffield was a rapidly expanding town with a population of 30,000. The water supply from a few small reservoirs at Crookesmoor was proving to be inadequate, and an act of parliament enabled the construction of the first Redmires Dam. Within 15 years the population had quadrupled, and a further two dams were sanctioned. It was the construction of these dams that led to two new beer houses opening on the moors. The opportunity to supplement incomes by brewing beer for the navvies was not one to miss, and the two neighbouring farms both obtained the £5 licences, issued under the Beer House Act, in order to cash in.

The beer houses were named the 'Grouse & Trout' and the 'Ocean View'. The naming of the former was in recognition of the shooting and fishing that was the lifeblood of the moor; presumably the owner of the latter had never before seen such a vast expanse of water as was developing outside his widows.

Both establishments commenced trading in the mid-1840s, and initially brewed their own beers. Hundreds of loud and often violent navvies descended on the beer houses and would often pass out in the barns and outbuildings rather than put up with the discomfort of the camps.

With the completion of the dams, roads had been built to enable construction materials to be brought to the site, and ramblers soon arrived to gaze at the new reservoirs and take in the spectacular views and fresh air that Stanage Edge offered.

The Ocean View called time in 1885, its landlord reverting to farming to make his living. The death of the Grouse & Trout was a more protracted affair. The landlord, Thomas Lowe, had already obtained a full public house licence. The end came as a result of quite unexpected circumstances.

By 1913 motor vehicles had arrived, and charabancs started to take the masses on to the moors to escape the pollution of the city. All this was too much for the moor's owner, who was frightened that poachers would be attracted to the pub and spoil his shooting. He demanded the licence be revoked from the Grouse & Trout, and such was the influence of landowners at the time, it was.

For years the Grouse & Trout carried on serving pots of tea and cakes, but eventually bowed to the inevitable. Following closure, the building was totally demolished. All that remains is a marker stone that had acted as the pub sign. It stands beside the road, bearing a carving of a grouse and three trout. There is a Latin inscription "Ich Dien Dinner" - I serve dinner. It is a testament to the pub that proved to be too successful for its own good.

My Kind of Picture

Bridge on the move

Having road and rail bridges right outside its doorway, there was no surprise when the pub at the bottom on Gleadless Road, Heeley, was named the Bridge Inn. What many folk are unaware of, however, is that the inn which stands alongside the River Sheaf is a replacement for one which was demolished in the early 1930s to allow for road widening. Here's the old (above) with the more familiar Bridge Inn (left) minus its signage.

How was your Sheffield childhood? Sybil O'Brien recalls that, for her, every day began with a proper breakfast and a dose of cod liver oil and malt. Supermarkets hadn't been invented and there were few cars on the streets, but her estate was visited by knife-sharpeners, the pop man, the bread man, the pikelet man and, of course, the rag man with balloons and goldfish to give away. Sybil talks to John Firminger

Days of innocence

Sybil O'Brien

IT was 26th April, 1950, at approximately 12.30am, when I arrived kicking and screaming into the world at 55 Scraith Wood Drive, Shirecliffe. I was helped on my way by our local GP and had my first bath in the bathroom sink, ably assisted by my Auntie Jen (my mother's youngest sister). This was how life would be in a prefab.

My dad, being the bread winner, had charge of all the money; I don't think my mum ever knew how much he earned. He gave her housekeeping every week and she had to manage the house, so when we needed new furniture it was a joint effort with the exception of the time he went out and bought an up-to-the-minute kitchen set comprising a table, chairs and a sideboard with a clock in the centre - all, I might add, in the brightest yellow and black flecked Formica. My mum hated it but never did tell him so that was our little secret. Mine was the fact I loved it, but I saw one recently in a retro shop and I have now revised my opinion - Mum was right.

Leading out of there at the other end was a door into the hallway. Here was the piano bought for my big brother who, incidentally, hated having lessons. Although I never said at the time, I would have loved to learn but girls had to do shorthand as a back-up plan, according to my dad, and he sent me off once a week to

private lessons to a big house in Walkley, two bus rides away in winter and I hated it. All I wanted to do at the time was to go out with my mates in my new Mary Quant black and white frock with matching ear-rings and knee boots. I thought I was the bee's knees.

If I tell you it was a community it would be undervaluing the life we had together on our estate - I suppose it could be described as a village - where everyone knew everyone else and their business. All the men had jobs and what a great diversity there was; we had postmen, nurses, mechanics, bus drivers and of course steelworkers, of which my dad was one.

Women didn't go out to work; they were "house technicians" - sorry, housewives - and they stayed home to look after the kids and tend the house with lots of endless, thankless jobs.

Oh I forgot, we did have a working woman but she was special. She was an actress her name was Mary Whetton (stage name Millar) and she travelled to London quite a lot. She later played Rose in the sit-com Keeping Up Appearances. She had a large white Samoyed dog that had hair you could spin. And I was a grateful recipient of a hat and scarf one Christmas made from said dog.

We walked to school after having a proper breakfast and a dose of cod liver oil and malt (yes you can still get it; I still take it now) and home again, changed into our playclothes and off we went adventuring.

I suppose we did have an advantage living in an ancient bluebell wood, complete with large oak trees, squirrels, foxes owls and a variety of wild birds most of which frequented our bird table. There were no discrimination or gender problems, we all played together either in our very large gardens or around the paths and interconnecting walkways.

Our garden had a distinct demarcation line, the back which comprised of a huge lawn complete with swing and play area and the washing line and around the front two separate gardens were divided by a path full of roses, carnations, bleeding heart, primroses and my Mum's pride and joy, two beautiful silver birch trees. We respected these and rarely played on them.

Most of the gardens were divided in a similar way, with the exception of the one belonging to Mr and Mrs Smith who lived on the end of our road and who had no kids. They had a huge privet hedge and a garden full of beautiful roses. At the height of summer we used to "dib" for who would knock on the door to ask for rose petals to make into perfume, boiling them in an old saucepan and decanting into jars to give away to family or whoever was daft enough to have them. Thinking about it now the smell was pretty rancid.

Because all of the kids played together, we had enough to play cowboys and Indians, building tents out of clothes-horses covered in utility blankets, and using our three-wheeled bikes as horses. We travelled far and wide on those summer evenings, playing out until it went dark or we got hungry, whichever came first.

You have to remember when we got in from school we had to have "us teas" first, usually meat and two veg with lashings of gravy. There was no "foreign muck" at our houses, only proper substantial food and a pudding, all sitting together at the table.

We built dens and dammed streams, we built mud pies and ate our fair share of muck; we even had fires in a small valley area away, of course, from the sight of our houses. I'm not sure if my mum ever knew about that! She would have killed me had she known.

We did grass sliding on cardboard boxes until the grass was bare and brown and picked bluebells for our bouquets when we were dressing up as princesses or May Queens. We collected jam-jars full of minnows and frogspawn and kept it on the kitchen window sill.

The seasons were apparent, spring brought the new growth bluebells and Whitsuntide clothes, summer with the endless school holidays, autumn with the conkers and acorns to collect - but now we just seem to have weather all year.

Winter was another cause for joy as when the snow came the community spirit became even closer, helping each other dig out and build snowmen and igloos. We all sledged together on big wooden contraptions with steel runners which froze solid with compacted snow and ice, lovingly made by our dads.

I loved playing out until it got dark with the street lamps glistening on the pure white snow a myriad of jewels for our benefit. We ate icicles from the roof because we could reach them, we caught large snowflakes on our tongues and scraped ice patterns from the inside of the windows - no double-glazing then - but we were all fit and healthy, wrapped up for the weather in our balaclavas with old socks on our hands after we wet our gloves snowballing.

Not many people had a car and there were no big supermarket chains. The mums had to go to town on the bus to do the shopping for fresh meat and veg, bread was baked at home, well in our house anyway, but we did have a variety of deliveries, Rington's Tea, the pop man, the bread man, a grocery van who sold everything you could ever want, a veritable mobile "Arkwrights" and of course the pikelet man on his bike with a basket on front. I can still hear his cry of "oatcakes and pikelets". They were a real treat for a big Sunday fry-up with black pudding, kidneys, liver, bacon, sausage, mushrooms and tomatoes.

The knife-sharpener also had a bike and the biggest treat of all was the rag man with his horse and cart and the promise of a balloon or a goldfish. I can't remember how many I had over the years or how long they lasted, I suspect a bit of jiggery pokery went on when I was at school swapping the dead fish for a live one carried home in a plastic bag on the bus by my loving mother.

The construction in the garden was big enough for coal but also a great storage area, once dad had erected shelves, for jars of stick insects, butterfly cocoons and elephant hawk moth caterpillars. Thinking about it now, that was the beginning of my love affair with nature. What a privileged life I had to have parents and a big brother who let me be myself and collect insects to study. My parents were, I suppose, unusual in that respect.

My mum had a love of opera and possessed a wonderful voice and our house was always full of singing and music of all genres from Sonny Boy Williamson to Terry Lightfoot and Flanagan and Allen. We spent time together listening to the wireless, even after we got the telly for the coronation.

Sunday was my favourite with The Billy Cotton Band Show, either The Navy Lark or Around the Horn. There was also Peter Brough and Archie Andrews, now what about that - listening to a ventriloquist on the wireless!

I listened to Benny Green, Alan Dell and Sing Something Simple all my adult life until one by one these entertainers died and Sundays have never been the same since. We all watched telly together as a treat and that is where I developed my passion for dancing. Even today I can tell you all the plots of every Fred Astaire film and the words to all of the songs - they don't make films like that today.

The community once again showed its true spirit when the Queen passed by the end of our road on her coronation tour. I remember sitting on my dad's shoulders waving a flag at a big black car driving down Herries Road and then having a big street party. I think it must have been 1955 but I'm not sure.

My Dad was a very special man too; he fought in World War II but never talked about it until one day, watching a programme on TV about Colditz, he announced he had been a prisoner of war there and had been relieved from there at the end of the war. The only thing he said about it was they all thought building the plane was bloody stupid because they never would have been able to get it out. He also said it was the best prisoner of war camp he had been in after Stalag 4B - funny how that name has stuck in my mind all of these years.

He also spent time with the Italian underground and never mentioned he could speak Italian until I had an Italian pen pal and he translated the letters for me - how embarrassing was that!

Dad taught me about yoga and spirituality and astral travelling, all things he had picked up in India, I don't think he ever mentioned them to anyone else, it was not the done thing for a steel-chipper to believe in life after death. All of these things have been a foundation for my life as it is today, based on an idyllic childhood living in a Sheffield Prefab.

• We would be delighted to learn about your childhood days in Sheffield. Why not share your memories with other readers of this publication? Write to My Kind of Town, 24 Hutcliffe Wood Road, Beauchief, Sheffield, S8 0EX, or email us at mike@heronpublications.co.uk

Gloss and guitars

John Carrack tells John Firminger about his double life as a musician and decorating shop proprietor. He also happens to be the elder brother of one of Britain's most popular singer songwriters

Paul started his musical career as a member of the Saville Row Rhythm Unit along with cousin Robert Batty on bass (left) and John Whitham (right) on guitar

THE next time you're in Crookes and you happen to call in at Carrack's Decorators' Supplies to buy a tin of paint or roll of wallpaper, you might also hear the sound of a guitar being played. This could well be the proprietor and part-time musician, the affable John Carrack.

"There's always a ukulele or a guitar hanging up in the shop; a lot of people who come in are also interested in guitar music," says John.

Carrack & Son is a long established name in the trade and having run the business since the early 1960s, John remembers back to when the shop was also the family home

"My dad went out decorating and my mum looked after the shop," he recalls.

At 15, John had left Weston Road School and had been working at Firth Brown's for six months, but would become involved in the family business as a result of a great tragedy.

"My dad had an accident and fell down a staircase and broke his neck, which was on Valentine's Day. This was on Thursday and on Sunday morning he died. Then they didn't really know how to deal with that sort of injury, like they would do now. He was 50 when he died."

This naturally left John, his mother and younger brother totally devastated: "We were really lucky that we had such a good family and my grandma came to stay with us all through that period."

Whilst young brother Paul recalled that for him it was a very insecure time, John, being older, managed to stay more positive.

"I'd got another four years on my back and also the strength of the family background on my mum's side. They were great and they dragged us through it."

John and Paul's dad had been a very popular figure with everyone around him, but his death also uncovered a secret: "I found out that my dad had been married before and was going to tell me but didn't. It's a bit like 'Living Years', the story really. I only found out after he'd died he'd been married before; there were no other children. And then he met my mum and we had a really great family life."

After temporarily helping out in the shop, John decided to work there permanently.

"The decorating ceased and the shop carried on. I'd never thought about working in that shop, but I started to enjoy it."

Something else that John has enjoyed for a long time is music, and is of course, the elder brother of the acclaimed singer/songwriter Paul Carrack.

"The musical side comes from my dad, although my grandma on my mum's side could sing really well. She'd got a little bit of Irish in her. My dad played drums and was in a little bit of a dance band."

John also recalls how some of the sounds of the 1950s first caught his ear: "The family all had Everly Brothers and Charlie Gracie records, 78s, and they had a massive radiogram and that sparked it off."

However, like his brother, it was the 1960s that provided John with some real musical inspiration, becoming particularly interested in the music of The Beatles. He then took a particular liking to acoustic music.

"I used to go to the Highcliffe (Hotel) a lot and I liked a lot of folk stuff: Bob Dylan and the Peter, Paul & Mary stuff, the more gentle stuff."

John recalls the first musical instrument he and his brother learned to play, a Bon Tempe keyboard that stood on four screw-in legs with one octave and it was a Christmas present. Paul was about eight when we had that and we had to share it."

Paul then took an interest in drums with his first kit being an ex-Salvation Army set his dad bought for him for a fiver. It included a very big bass drum with the Salvation Army Crest on it.

"When he sat down to play them you couldn't see him at all!"

Musically-minded, the two had a variety of instruments, including a zither.

"We had all sorts of stuff; the upstairs part of the shop we had was like a den, so we used to bash about up there. The first Christmas

My Kind of People

Seeing double. The Carrack brothers on stage Sheffield City Hall... but who's got the cherry?

after my dad died, my mum bought Paul a complete set of Trixon drums which she took a loan out for. She gave both of us a great Christmas after he'd died."

As a young drummer, Paul started his musical career as a member of the Saville Row Rhythm Unit along with cousin Robert Batty on bass and John Whitham on guitar with regular bookings at the County Hotel on Howard Street.

Like many others his age, John's musical interest was the guitar.

"Just before my dad died, I had one for Christmas. It was a Futurama and cost 25 guineas from Milners. It was brand new and was red but I couldn't afford an amplifier so we played it though an Elizabethan tape recorder. That started us off and we shared it. I swopped it for a Vox and I wish I hadn't done - I wish I'd still got it. Then I bought an amplifier. I got a speaker from somebody and it was full of concrete and I could hardly carry it!"

Progressing musically, Paul became a member of soul band CG Morris and The Reaction and switched to keyboard.

"They used to practice in the shop. My mum bought a house on St Anthony's Road so the back of the shop was free and was full of all their stuff."

John recalls how the band also brought along some uninvited guests to the shop: "The stuff had been at Clive's for a week and came back full of mice, so the shop was full of them!"

Free of mice, CG Morris & Reaction with its featured brass section became quite successful, playing clubs and dances. Paul also began to develop as a singer, but nearly didn't due to brother John.

"We used to fall out over the daftest things. Saturday night we used to have a cherry bun, just a little cake with icing and a cherry. I used to take my cherry off and leave it while last. I turned round to look at something and he picked it up and had it. So then we started wrestling and I covered him up with a cushion and nearly bloody choked him!".

Seemingly, the brothers are still disagreeing over that cherry today!

The 1960s saw Paul leave home and hit the road. John recalls: "He had a job at the Gas Board from school then got an opportunity with some other lads from Burnley and they went to Hamburg. So he was in Germany when he was 16. My mum must have gone through some sleepless nights back then."

Indeed for Paul's mum, the life of a professional musician must have been hard to come to terms with and she always used to tell him to "get a proper job".

John Carrack: 'We used to fall out over the daftest things'

Maintaining his own interest music, John bought his first acoustic guitar, a Gibson, in 1964 and at a bargain price.

"Phil Robinson phoned and said there was a Gibson in Bradley's for £45. It was Saturday afternoon and I went straight down and got it. I had £20 of my own, my mom gave me a tenner and my grandma gave me £15."

John still has the instrument which now stands proudly in his home as part of a small collection of Gibson acoustic guitars.

"Anything strung, I've got a five-string banjo and a tenor banjo and I love the ukulele."

This has led John to attend some of the George Formby nights which are held locally. He is also currently involved in a guitar night class held weekly at Walkley Community Centre.

"We hire a room for £14 for two hours. It started with seven of us and the average number is now about 15. I've encouraged a lot of people to come along."

Strangely enough, although John and his brother continue to share a great love for music, they've not got together to perform in recent times.

"Funnily enough, y'know, we haven't and when I go to his house we just sit on the settee and talk."

However, one thing that they did do together was appear on the City Hall stage in 2008. Done as a bit of a laugh, they both dressed the same, and performed Over My Shoulder.

"That was a very exciting night," John recalled, with great pride, adding: "And I never got paid either!"

Away from music and back in the shop, a particular funny incident that John remembers concerned a lady customer.

"The woman wanted to buy this wallpaper and we told her 'from this book, we can't send them back so if you order so many that's it.'

"We told her to go and do a little sketch, put her measurements on it, bring it back and we would try to work it out. So she came back with a detailed drawing, minute sizes for every nook and cranny, and every angle everywhere.

"We went through all this and said 'well, there's a match on this paper so I think you'll need seven rolls.' Then she told us: 'It only took six last time'!"

So whether it be a tin of paint, learning to play a guitar or simply for a laugh, John's shop is always an interesting place to call in.

The Village Hall time travellers

Barlborough folk know the secret of how to travel back in time... they simply play the music which had everyone rockin' on the dancefloor at their 1960s Youth Club nights. John Firminger joins them on one of their most nostalgic evenings to date

JUST like the Law, My Kind Of Town has a long arm and reaches out to some of Sheffield's periphery as we head south to visit the sleepy village of Barlborough.

Actually, sleepy might not be so applicable (well not always) as back in February, it was anything but, as the windows of the old Village Hall rattled and the dance floor creaked to the sounds of rock 'n' roll once again. Such a break in the usual peace and quiet saw the patrons of the still occasionally active Barlborough Youth Club turn back the years and celebrate its 50th anniversary.

Starting off in the late 1950s, the club was galvanised around 1961 with the advent of the beat boom as Barlborough Youth Club became just as much a part of the swingin' scene as anywhere else.

Of course, a major part of the club's original activities was music with the weekly gathering generally gravitating towards the club's state-of-the-art Volmar record player. In charge of such a focal piece of equipment would usually be Ken Robinson who would spin the latest platters (to use some vernacular of the day) whilst he and the rest of the members would listen to the various releases and discuss their merits or otherwise.

In this capacity the club actually took part in one of the 'Juke Box Jury' sessions that The Star's monthly supplement, Top Stars Special, would organise around the various local youth clubs, publishing the panel's views on a batch of new releases.

Looking back through the archives,

Dean and Chris Jade with The Originals at Barlborough

Barlborough rose to the occasion and their deliberations provided a most entertaining read. Ken recalled the club's most popular 'platter' was the instrumental Last Date by Floyd Cramer, usually played at the end of an evening; it sent the members home with a nice romantic glow.

As well as the music on disc, the club would also feature regular live music with numerous bands booked to appear there. Some of the groups who kept the young guys 'n' gals hoppin 'n' boppin' included The Crestas, The Vantennas, The Cadillacs, Jimmy Crawford, The Fentones, The Originals with vocal duo Chris and Dean Jade (formerly Mickey and Johnnie) and Joe Cocker just prior to his great success with The Grease Band.

Back then the club boasted a 150-strong membership but this accumulated when the club began putting bands on, with patrons coming from a wide surrounding area.

Another act offered to the club was American singer Bruce Channell accompanied by harmonica player Delbert McClinton for £100. Unfortunately the club had to decline as paying out such an astronomical fee back then would have been too much for them to risk.

One celebrity who did visit the club was film actress Ingrid Hafner who starred in the first series of The Avengers. As the niece of the local vicar, Ingrid was invited to attend the club and did so on several other occasions.

Enjoying great popularity in the mid 60s, the club had various agents phoning up wanting to book their bands in. The club also

BARLBOROUGH COUNTY YOUTH CENTRE

Radio, T.V. and Parlophone Recording Stars

presents on the stage

THE FENTONES

FRIDAY, JULY 16th

Non-Stop Dancing from 7-30 pm to 10-30 pm

No Pass Outs   Doors Close 9 p.m.

Tickets 2/6

(Members and Invited Guests Only)

Right: Dave Berry and
The Cruisers had a date
at a Barlborough Youth
Club dance in 1962

Below right: A
Barlborough Youth
Club ticket from two
years later

BARLBOROUGH YOUTH CLUB
Details of Dances for April 1962

FRIDAY 6th   7 p.m. to 10 p.m.
EDDIE FALCON & THE TREMORS

FRIDAY 13th   7 p.m. to 10 p.m.
DAVE BETTON & THE BARRYTONES

EASTER MONDAY
23rd APRIL   7 p.m. to 10-30 p.m.
JOHNNY DARK & THE MIDNIGHTERS

FRIDAY 27th   7 p.m to 10 p.m.
THE FABULOUS
DAVE BERRY & THE CRUISERS

ADMISSION to each of the above Dances
MEMBERS 2/-
GUESTS   3/-

In each case, selections of Top British and American
Records will be featured, and a Prize will be given to the
lucky Ticket Holder.

LIGHT REFRESHMENTS ALSO AVAILABLE

Printed by Raymond Walkley, Eckington

had its own drama group and in March 1964 their production
of the farce 'As Long As They're Happy' was their contribution
to the North East Derbyshire Youth Club
Drama Festival.

More recognition came that year when member
Margaret Owen won the Miss Clubland contest which
was held between all the North East Derbyshire youth
clubs. Tragically, Margaret died in 1969 from cancer
but her achievement is still fondly remembered.

The music of the 60s, and the part it played at the
club, left such strong memories that it seemed like a good
idea to turn back the clock and relive some of those
times. Some of the surviving members had occasional
get-togethers, recalling when they were all young and
innocent (or so they tell us).

In an effort to recreate those days, former club
member Susan Fazackerley put the idea forward to
hold a reunion night. After recruiting fellow ex-members
Fred Rodgers, Malc Gregory and Ken Robinson - all
of whom were equally enthusiastic about the idea - it
was put into operation with the first reunion night
staged in 2009 taking place back in the club's old
premises, the Village Hall.

The event was a great success with a very
encouraging turnout as many more old members of
the village youth club came out of the woodwork to
join in the fun. With a craving for more, the committee
followed it up with another similar bash.

Making a perfect contribution towards these journeys back in time have
been local band Past Masters. Now celebrating their own tenth year
together, this bunch of ace veteran rockers recreate those vintage sounds
perfectly. Their participation at these revived club nights have certainly
fuelled this friendly time-machine.

For the 50th anniversary of when the club really took off, the committee
felt that they needed to hold a special night that would mark its
significance. Providing the perfect solution were local heroes, Dave Berry
and The Cruisers

BARLBOROUGH COUNTY YOUTH CENTRE
invites you to
STOMP 'N' SHAKE
to the sound of the FABULOUS
TONY WILD & THE DRUMBEATS
FRIDAY, 3rd APRIL, 1964
7.30 p.m. — 10.30 p.m.

Tickets 2/6   Members and Invited Guests only
No Passouts   Doors close 9 p.m.

Youth Club
members dancing
to the band

A proud moment for Barlborough and its Youth Club as Margaret Owen receives her award as Miss Clubland

BARLBOROUGH YOUTH CLUB
DETAILS OF
DANCES FOR MAY 1962

FRIDAY 4th   7 p.m. to 10 p.m.
BY POPULAR DEMAND — A RETURN VISIT OF
JOHNNY AND THE CRESTAS

FRIDAY 11th   7 p.m. to 10 p.m.
THE SENSATIONAL
CADILLACS
(WINNERS OF THE BIG BEAT COMPETITION RECENTLY
HELD AT HANDSWORTH PLAZA, SHEFFIELD)

FRIDAY 18th   7 p.m. to 10 p.m.
THE FABULOUS
RADIO, T.V. AND COLUMBIA RECORDING ARTISTES
JIMMY CRAWFORD and the RAVENS
(HIT RECORDERS OF "I LOVE HOW YOU LOVE ME")
Admission   Members 3/-   Guests 4/-

FRIDAY 25th   7 p.m. to 10 p.m.
THE FIRST VISIT BY
JOHNNY HAWK & the FALCONS

IN EACH CASE, SELECTIONS OF TOP BRITISH AND
AMERICAN RECORDS WILL BE FEATURED, AND A PRIZE
WILL BE GIVEN TO THE HOLDER OF THE LUCKY TICKET.

LIGHT REFRESHMENTS WILL ALSO BE AVAILABLE

Prices of Admission
(EXCEPT WHERE OTHERWISE SHOWN)
MEMBERS 2/-   GUESTS 3/-

who had in fact performed at the club way back in 1962. Ken Robinson has proof of the gig with a receipt for £20, the agreed fee for Dave and the band to appear.

Following talks with Dave, he was only too pleased to fix up a return gig at the club's anniversary reunion, although his fee had of course by now increased slightly from the original booking.

With everything in place, Dave and The Cruisers' appearance at the Barlborough Youth Club Reunion on 12th February, 2011, was a great success with the Village Hall packed to capacity. My Kind Of Town was there too, mingling with old club members and some of the other faithful fans who support Dave's local gigs.

On stage Dave recalled the time he originally played at the club and said jokingly that he must have gone down well because it had only taken the organisers 49 years to re-book him!

Along with the music and the club's very friendly atmosphere, the night brought back those times when everybody looked much younger and thankfully, there were no mirrors around to shatter the illusion as they recalled some of their misspent youth.

• Do you have any special youth club memories? If so let us know - we might even be prepared to change the names to protect the innocent!

Left: A club flyer from 1962 promising a great night out for three bob.

Right: Dave Berry must have gone down well in the village because he was invited back there just 49 years later

Ken Robinson and Joan Bunting spin the wax (we mean play the records)

It's Memory Lane

Some mighty big changes were happening at Sheffield United's Bramall Lane ground in the summer of 1994

My Kind of Photos

WELCOME to beautiful downtown Bramall Lane... as you've never seen it before.

Many people will know that the famous old stadium suffered a direct hit in the Sheffield Blitz, but these pictures were taken as recently as 1994. That year saw the demolition of the John Street stand which had looked down on not only football, but county cricket too.

'My Kind of Town' journalist Mike Firth recalls he was working on a local newspaper at the time and was at Sheffield United to cover the story of a summer signing. Looking out across the playing surface, he couldn't believe the scene.

"The final sections of the old stand were being flattened and smoke was coming from a couple of fires which the demolition men had lit," he says. "But not only that, all the grass had gone too; it was a real dustbowl."

The first of the ground's five floodlight pylons had also been demolished and work was beginning to install seating beneath the stand at the Bramall Lane end of the ground.

Down crashes the old stand as sprinklers try to encourage new grass to grow on the pitch

More pictures of the demolition in progress and (right) a reminder of how the old John Street stand had looked

When the FA gave in to Sheffield

The Football Association is not renowned for relenting in the face of fan power but it did just that following an outcry from Sheffield supporters in 1993. Mike Firth explains

JUST one look at the football programme opposite will bring a smile to one half of Sheffield... and remind others of a chilling disappointment.

It is a souvenir of the glorious day in April 1993 when Sheffield produced two successful football teams which met in a semi-final of the FA Cup at Wembley. The fact that 75,364 people travelled to Wembley for the game is part of the city's folklore, but what may have been forgotten by some is that the FA initially planned to stage the Sheffield showcase at, of all places, Leeds United's Elland Road ground. Whatever the result, it just would not have been the same, would it?

There was a city-wide outcry when the original planned venue was announced and the fax machine at FA headquarters was jammed with protests from Owls and Blades fans. The other semi was to be played at Wembley, so why not ours too?

Editing a local paper at the time, I was one of the people to contact the FA over the matter. I can't recall what surprised me most, whether it was the FA eventually seeing sense and relenting to everyone's wishes or receiving a personal reply from FA chief executive Graham Kelly!

I've kept the letter and match programme as souvenirs... and sometimes wonder if it was my complaint which got Sheffield to Wembley!

THE FOOTBALL ASSOCIATION
LIMITED
Founded 1863

Patron: HER MAJESTY THE QUEEN
President: H.R.H. THE DUKE OF KENT
Chairman: SIR BERT MILLICHIP

Chief Executive:
R. H. G. KELLY FCIS

Phone: 071-402 7151/071-262 4542
Telex: 261110
Facsimile: 071-402 0486

16 LANCASTER GATE, LONDON W2 3LW

Our Ref:
RHGK/vmc/144

Your Ref:

5th April 1993

Dear Mr. Firth,

~~Thank you for writing to us about the venue for the FA Cup~~ semi-final tie between Sheffield United and Sheffield Wednesday.

You will, I am sure, be aware that the game ~~will now~~ *was* be played at Wembley Stadium on Saturday, April 3, kick-off 1.00 pm, with a replay if necessary on Wednesday, April 7 at Old Trafford.

The usual criteria for selecting a semi-final venue is the nearest suitable neutral venue to the competing clubs; hence the decision to use Wembley for the Arsenal v Tottenham Hotspur tie and Elland Road for the Sheffield game.

However, we have listened to the strong feelings expressed by the supporters of both Sheffield clubs and of the clubs themselves and feel that their wish to play at Wembley should be granted. We were also mindful that comments made could have incited problems on the day had the game remained at Elland Road despite the confidence of the Leeds authorities to manage the game.

I do hope you enjoyed the match.

Yours sincerely,

Chief Executive

Registered Office: 16 Lancaster Gate, London W2 3LW
Incorporated in London   Registration Number 77797

F.A. CUP SEMI-FINAL
SATURDAY 3 APRIL 1993

SHEFFIELD

UNITED

v

SHEFFIELD

WEDNESDAY

KICK - OFF 1.00 P.M.

OFFICIAL MATCHDAY PROGRAMME £4.00

Mr Manton's history class

From Romans to Roundheads to rare FA Cup successes, Dafydd Manton (pictured) takes a quirkly look at the Sheffield story

BLAME it on the Brigantes. After all, the Romans did, and I wouldn't want to argue with the likes of Tiberius Claudius Caesar Augustus Germanicus, if only because it just took five minutes to type his name. That he died on 13th October 54 AD is another good reason why argument would be fruitless.

However, he it was who ordered the invasion of Britain, for reasons that nobody has ever successfully explained. It can't have been the strategic importance of our little island for deploying forward air power, because however far-sighted Tiberius might have been, predicting the advent of the jet fighter would have been stretching things a bit. So, let us look at the background.

The Catuvellauni had displaced the Trinovantes as the most powerful kingdom, and had taken over Camulodunum, as you would expect. They were pressing their neighbours the Atribates under Commius, formerly mates with Julius Caesar. I need hardly remind you that Dumnovellaunus and Tincomarus had already legged it to Rome, so Tiberius brought in Aulus Plautius, with Vespasian, Gnaeus Hosidius Geta, Titus Flavius Sabinus II, Dio Cassius and Gnaeus Sentius Saturninus under him. Rumour has it there was also a leader called Dubuldeckerus Bus, but historians Eutropius and Suetonius don't say much. Suetonius is better known as Atora.

As you can imagine, if you'd spent your entire life in a pile of stones just outside Totley, all these strange names were unnecessarily hard work, and so the Brigantes capitulated, although they didn't realise it at the time. They thought they were putting in an order for takeaway pizza. The fact that Sheffield, like Rome, is built on seven hills is coincidence at best. Rome boasts the Colosseum, the Pantheon, the Arch of Constantine and the Forum Trajanum, but they haven't got Meadowhall or Abbeydale Industrial Hamlet.

From the Roman invasion, which almost by-passed Sheffield, much like the M1, to the 19th Century, very little happened. In fact, what is now a thriving city and centre of Asian cuisine was once a field by the River Sheaf. Sheaf Field - Sheffield. Simple. It is no secret that little happens in the average field, and that which does is not suitable for an august publication such as this. For that sort of thing, try reading Farmers' Weekly, a popular publication since MCMXXXIV.

Admittedly, the castle was built, a Motte and Bailey construction which was destroyed in 1264, as a result of the Second Baron's War. This was a replay after extra time of the First Baron's War. The castle was rebuilt as a stone structure in 1270, apparently by a gentleman by the name of William de Lovetot, who must have been a gift to any Tudor comedians. Mary Queen of Scots was imprisoned here, between 1570 and 1584, although to be fair, practically every building between Land's End and John o'Groats that was standing in the 16th century has made the same claim, as well as quite a few that were built hundreds of years later. If Mary had made every tapestry that has been claimed, she would have worked 24 hours a day for 319 years, assuming that you could get the candles. She eventually lost her head in 1587, thanks to the kind ministrations of her first cousin, Elizabeth I. Next time you have a family squabble about where you are going to spend the next Bank Holiday, remember poor dear Mary.

The castle also featured in the Civil War, being the centre for a punch-up between the Roundheads and the Cavaliers. The Cavaliers would appear to have been the more popular, if only because there is no such thing as a Roundhead King Charles Spaniel, or a Vauxhall Roundhead. That didn't stop the Roundheads winning, and the castle was handed over to them in 1644, and became one of the ruins that Cromwell knocked about a bit. Well, a lot actually, as it disappeared. It suffered the ultimate fate in 1927, when the Brightside & Carbrook Co-op was built on top of it. As you wander down the aisles looking for the value baked beans, you can still hear the clank of armour, although it's more likely a truck delivering another consignment of Spam.

Of course, mention the name Sheffield, and the first thing people think about is steel, unless you are a United supporter who remembers the 1925 FA Cup (1-0 against Cardiff) or a Wednesday fan who was around in 1935 when they lifted the Cup following a 4-2 victory over West Bromwich Albion. The best steel in the world has been made in the city since the 14th century, as well as the world-famous Sheffield Plate. This is not a tennis trophy, although possibly tennis trophies have been made of Sheffield plate. It is a layering of copper and silver, discovered entirely by accident by Thomas Boulsover in 1743. Don't you just love that it was pure chance, rather than years of experimentation, trial, laboratory work, burning the midnight oil and poring over a thousand books. Somehow, it makes Mr Boulsover seem a bit more accessible and a bit less like a stern-faced individual in a powdered wig. Not, of course, that it is particularly easy to take a man in a wig too seriously to begin with.

The Sheffield steel industry flourished in the period 1914-1918 and 1939 -1945. To say anything more would be in poor taste.

The heyday of Sheffield lasted well in to the 1970s. It is an emotive period, with the miners' strikes of 1972, 1974 and 1984. Just as an aside, the strike of '72 was the first miners' strike since 1926, which is probably better than most industries. The effectiveness of the strikes is a moot point, but with his hairstyle, Arthur Scargill did much to popularise Shredded Wheat.

However, the post-war period did bring about one change, in that photography became ever more popular, and available to the masses. As a result, there is a great social history archive, the beginnings of which you hold e'en now in your warm little hands. They say that a picture is worth a thousand words. Just think, instead of all this text, they could have simply printed one photograph. Time to shut up, methinks.